Access to History

General Editor: Keith Randell

Britain: Industrial Relations and the Economy 1900–39

Robert Pearce

Hodder & Stoughton

A MEMBER OF THE HODDER HEADLINE GROUP

The cover illustration is a portrait of Ernest Bevin by Thomas Cantrell Dugdale, 1945 (Courtesy National Portrait Gallery)

Some other titles in the series:

Britain: Domestic Politics, 1918–39 Robert Pearce	ISBN 0 340 55647 1
Britain: Foreign and Imperial Affairs 1919–39 Alan Farmer	ISBN 0 340 55928 4
Labour and Reform: Working Class Movements, 1815–1914 Clive Behagg	ISBN 0 340 52930 X
Italy: Liberalism and Fascism, 1870–1945 Mark Robson	ISBN 0 340 54548 8
Germany: The Third Reich, 1933–45 Geoff Layton	ISBN 0 340 53847 3

Order: Please contact Bookpoint Ltd, 39 Milton Park, Abingdon, Oxon OX14 4TD. Telephone: (44) 01235 400414. Fax: (44) 01235 400454. Lines are open from 9 am - 6 pm Monday to Saturday, with a 24-hour message answering service. Email address: orders@bookpoint.co.uk

British Library Cataloguing in Publication Data

Pearce, Robert D.
   Britain: Industrial Relations and the
   Economy, 1900-39.- (Access to History
   Series)
  I.Title   II. Series
   941.082

ISBN 0 340 57374 0

First published 1993

Impression number	13 12 11 10 9 8 7 6 5 4
Year	2004 2003 2002 2001 2000 1999 1998

Copyright © 1993 Robert Pearce

Typeset by Wearset, Boldon, Tyne and Wear.
Printed in Great Britain for Hodder & Stoughton Educational,
a division of Hodder Headline Plc, 338, Euston Road, London NW1 3BH
by Redwood Books, Trowbridge, Wiltshire.

Contents

Preface

To the general reader

Although the *Access to History* series has been designed with the needs of students studying the subject at higher examination levels very much in mind, it also has a great deal to offer the general reader. The main body of the text (i.e. ignoring the Study Guides at the ends of chapters) forms a readable and yet stimulating survey of a coherent topic as studied by historians. However, each author's aim has not merely been to provide a clear explanation of what happened in the past (to interest and inform): it has also been assumed that most readers wish to be stimulated into thinking further about the topic and to form opinions of their own about the significance of the events that are described and discussed (to be challenged). Thus, although no prior knowledge of the topic is expected on the reader's part, she or he is treated as an intelligent and thinking person throughout. The author tends to share ideas and possibilities with the reader, rather than passing on numbers of so-called 'historical truths'.

To the student reader

There are many ways in which the series can be used by students studying History at a higher level. It will, therefore, be worthwhile thinking about your own study strategy before you start your work on this book. Obviously, your strategy will vary depending on the aim you have in mind, and the time for study that is available to you.

If, for example, you want to acquire a general overview of the topic in the shortest possible time, the following approach will probably be the most effective:

1 Read chapter 1 and think about its contents.
2 Read the 'Making notes' section at the end of chapter 2 and decide whether it is necessary for you to read this chapter.
3 If it is, read the chapter, stopping at each heading or ★ to note down the main points that have been made.
4 Repeat stage 2 (and stage 3 where appropriate) for all the other chapters.

If, however, your aim is to gain a thorough grasp of the topic, taking however much time is necessary to do so, you may benefit from carrying out the same procedure with each chapter, as follows:

1 Read the chapter as fast as you can, and preferably at one sitting.
2 Study the flow diagram at the end of the chapter, ensuring that you understand the general 'shape' of what you have just read.

3 Read the 'Making notes' section (and the 'Answering essay questions' section, if there is one) and decide what further work you need to do on the chapter.

4 Attempt the 'Source-based questions' section. It will sometimes be sufficient to think through your answers, but additional understanding will often be gained by forcing yourself to write them down.

When you have finished the main chapters of the book, study the 'Further Reading' section and decide what additional reading (if any) you will do on the topic.

This book has been designed to help make your studies both enjoyable and successful. If you can think of ways in which this could have been done more effectively, please write to tell me. In the meantime, I hope that you will gain greatly from your study of History.

Keith Randell

CHAPTER 1

Introduction

Those who have never studied British history from 1900 to 1939 may nevertheless be inclined to think that they understand this period. So strong are 'folk memories' from the past that everyone, in the field of industrial relations, has heard of the General Strike of 1926, when almost the entire population took sides in the most spectacular industrial dispute in British history. Industrial relations are popularly supposed, on the basis of this event, to have amounted to little more than bitter and sterile confrontation. Similarly British economic performance over the same period is generally seen as a process of dismal decline. No particular event stands out: instead, a whole decade is remembered. The 1930s are enshrined in the popular consciousness as 'a low, dishonest decade', 'the devil's decade', powerfully symbolised by the dole queue and the hunger marches. The Thirties are seen as both the worst decade of the period and yet, at the same time, as in some way typical of a much longer time-span.

Readers, at this stage, may be excused for supposing that this is going to be a pessimistic and rather depressing book! But in fact these 'folk memories' are very limited and one-sided interpretations of the past, demonstrating the truth of the oft-quoted assertion that 'a little learning is a dangerous thing'. Indeed popular images of the past often hinder true understanding. Such myths are difficult to dispel, but historians must try to put aside preconceptions and penetrate to the reality of the past – which is always more varied and more interesting than any simple, single image. But before we look at 1900–39 we must review the nineteenth century. For just as we cannot understand the present without knowing the past, so we cannot understand any period of the past without understanding *its* historical background.

1 The Nineteenth-century Economy

In the middle of the nineteenth century Britain was the world's strongest economic power. Already, from about 1760, the country had undergone substantial economic growth: the power of the water wheel had been harnessed to drive cotton spinning machinery, with a resulting massive increase in the output of the textile industry. Then, in the first half of the nineteenth century, the steam engine had been used to supply an even greater motive power to machines. As a result, Britain became the 'workshop of the world'. Many historians have recently criticised the use of the term 'industrial revolution' to describe this process because it seems to imply a more rapid and complete economic change than in fact occurred, and their point of view is supported by the fact that much of Britain remained relatively immune to the growth of industry and saw continuity as well as change. However, it remains true that large parts of Britain were dramatically transformed by industrialisation, as was the country's place in the world economy.

In the middle of the nineteenth century Britain produced two-thirds of the world's coal, half the world's iron, five-sevenths of its steel, and half its cotton goods. Britain was exporting far more than any other nation and was also importing more food and raw materials. A country with only two per cent of the world's population was producing a staggering 40 per cent of the world's manufactured goods. Britain's economic strength lay primarily in its so-called 'staple industries' – textiles, coal, iron and steel, and shipbuilding – while the financial, banking and insurance services offered by the City of London further added to the strength and profitability of the economy.

The supposed causes of this economic success did not for long escape the penetrating eye of the Victorians. It appeared obvious to them that it was due to their own inventiveness, skill and capacity for hard work; in short to their innate, all-round superiority! No doubt they were God's new chosen people. Historians, however, have seen it rather differently. Most have argued that industrialisation was caused by a complex combination of factors (including population growth, the availability of capital, and technological inventions) simply coming together in Britain first. Britain's industrial supremacy over other countries in the mid-nineteenth century was, in the words of one historian, largely a 'happy accident'. Britain was the world's *first* industrial nation, and it achieved a substantial lead not because it was 'better' than other countries but simply because it began the race before its potential competitors were even at the starting line.

This economic growth affected the way of life of most of Britain's population. A basically agrarian society gave way to an industrial one. In 1851, for the first time, just over 50 per cent of the population of England and Wales lived in urban rather than rural areas, and by 1901 over 75 per cent lived in towns. The most characteristic form of employment became factory labour, and as the century proceeded a growing sense of 'class identity' occurred. At the start of the century most 'workers' had no consciousness of being part of the same group, but by about 1900 a greater cohesion was beginning to appear. The British population was made up of a small landed aristocracy (the traditional rulers of agrarian society), the middle classes (the owners and managers of the factories, as well as the traders and professionals) and, the largest group of all, the working *classes* – the plural being preferred to the singular because of the wide variations in pay that existed amongst wage-earners. Some skilled workers could earn a very good living, but for most unskilled workers – who might have to work for 15 hours at a stretch during 'brisk' times – wages were often appallingly low. On average 'real wages' (that is, wages in relation to prices, or 'purchasing power') per head of the population in Britain quadrupled during the nineteenth century, but not everyone shared equally in this growing prosperity. As a result of extensive research, Seebohm Rowntree established in 1899 that a third of the population of York lived in poverty, since the wages of an unskilled labourer were insufficient to keep a family 'in a state of bare physical efficiency'. Many workers complained of gross exploitation by their employers. Some thought that a violent revolution would be necessary to end this state of affairs, but far more turned for help to trade unions.

2 Nineteenth-century Trade Unionism

Trade unionism achieved substantial success during the nineteenth century. Yet no one in 1800 could have predicted the growth that was to occur. Indeed in this year unions were illegal, such 'combinations' being associated with the revolutionary ideas current across the Channel in the homeland of Britain's enemy, France. Although the legal ban was removed in 1824, the nature of legitimate trade union activity – of what, in law, unions should be allowed to do – was still a matter for controversy, and indeed has remained so ever since. Yet whatever the legal position, many employers simply refused to recognise the existence of trade unions amongst their employees and would not bargain with them. Partly as a result of this, trade unions were slow to develop and did so in piecemeal fashion. Only in the 1850s did they make significant progress.

In 1851 the Amalgamated Society of Engineers (ASE) was founded, with engineers throughout the country coming together to press for improvements in their industry. It turned out to be only the first of a group referred to by some historians as the 'new model unions'. The ASE and its imitators were 'craft' unions, combinations of highly skilled and well-paid men, sometimes called the 'labour aristocracy'. They were exclusive organisations, only open to particular workers, their aims being to maintain or increase their own wage levels, to improve their conditions of work and also to ensure that only men with their own skills could enter their particular trade. Membership fees were usually high, providing not only for the employment of full-time union officials but for sick pay, funeral expenses and other benefits. Members of these unions did not believe in general working-class solidarity, and although a few unions for less skilled workers did exist in this period the great bulk of unskilled and semi-skilled men and women did not belong to any union.

During the third quarter of the nineteenth century the economy expanded rapidly and trade unionism made significant advances. Membership rose from about 100,000 in 1850 to more than one million in 1875, and in 1869 the Trades Union Congress (TUC) was formed to give a collective voice to the craft unions. Nevertheless, commentators judged that the main weakness of the movement was still the paucity of unskilled and semi-skilled members, and the period after 1875 seemed to provide difficult conditions for further expansion. Membership declined substantially as the economy contracted. Even so, important developments took place from the late 1880s. In 1888 several union leaders called for the unionisation of all workers, and over the next few years the 'new unions' emerged. These organisations differed from the old craft unions: they admitted unskilled and semi-skilled workers and were 'general' unions, embracing all workers in a particular industry and not just those men and women performing the same functions. Almost immediately they proved their power, winning two well-publicised strikes – the match girls' strike in 1888 and the London dock strike in the following year. After this boost to workers' aspirations union growth proceeded apace, and even white-collar workers formed their own organisations.

In 1900 there were about two million trade union members, and the movement was much stronger than ever before. Yet trade unionism still had noticeable points of weakness. Despite the advances of the late nineteenth century, most trade unionists were still skilled or semi-skilled men, so that the great majority of male workers – who were unskilled – did not belong to a union and only three per cent of women workers were members. In total, no more than about 15 per cent of all workers were unionised, and still only a minority of employers would recognise and negotiate with them. Furthermore, politicians had yet to make up their minds whether to treat the unions as friend or foe.

3 The Role of Governments

a) Official Attitudes to Trade Unions

Governments tended to be uncertain about how to react to trade unions and, as a result, their position in law was not clearly defined. In 1824 Parliament gave unions legal recognition but failed to specify what they could and could not do. Once it became clear that the unions would not confine themselves to peaceful wage bargaining but would organise strikes, severe laws were passed against intimidation and obstruction during disputes. Hence, while government – through the law – was prepared to allow unions to exist, it was not prepared to allow them to mount effective strike action.

The 1870s saw several changes in the law. Legal protection was given to trade union funds, so that officials who stole their members' money could be punished, and, most important of all, 'peaceful picketing' was allowed for the first time. Whereas, a few years earlier, men and women had been arrested merely for shouting insults at those who worked during a strike, now only acts of physical violence were punishable by law. Politicians seemed prepared to tolerate, though not to encourage, the trade unions. Nevertheless their recognition of the unions was grudging, and as a result key issues were left undefined. Were unions immune to prosecutions from employers whose profits had declined because of 'industrial action'? Equally important, in what sense, if any, did unions have the right to involve themselves in politics? Could trade unions sponsor candidates at elections, and pay their salaries if they were elected to Parliament? The first trade union representative entered the House of Commons in 1874, duly elected by his constituents, but to some this seemed a dangerous portent of union power. By the end of the nineteenth century politicians had still not fully come to terms with trade unionism.

b) Official Attitudes to Finance and the Economy

Britain's spectacular industrial growth had not occurred as a result of government initiatives, and politicians therefore decided that they ought as far as possible to stand aside from economic affairs, pursuing a policy of *laissez-faire* (non-interventionism). But they could not totally detach themselves. They felt that they had to take action in some matters. First, in the area of social policy, they came to accept as the nineteenth century wore on that they had to do something about working conditions, for instance by specifying the maximum number of hours women and children could work. In addition, they had to take action to reduce the incidence of disease in Britain's cities and to provide some sort of relief for the 'deserving poor'. Secondly, they were concerned with 'finance', raising taxation to cover the costs of administration, social policy and defence. But they were determined not to hamstring industry by taxing it too heavily. The defence budget was therefore kept low, and governments were concerned to avoid wars. Peace was seen to be in the national interest. On the whole, it was generally believed that the less government, the better. If governments stood aside from the economy as much as possible, allowing individuals to pursue their own self-interest, the maximum degree of economic prosperity would be sure to result.

4 Twentieth-century Themes

History is so vast that we can never hope to study more than a fraction of it. This is especially true for the twentieth century, about which so much evidence survives. So which elements should we select for particular scrutiny? Obviously, there is no 'correct' answer to this question. Some themes seem to select themselves because they were so important in the past, while others are often chosen because they seem relevant and topical today. Those who look into the past often see a reflection of the issues and priorities current in their own times. Perhaps this is inevitable, but we should be on our guard lest present concerns lead us to distort the past by giving undue prominence to some aspects of it.

a) Trade Union Issues

Historians of the period 1900–39 have focused on several issues relating to trade unions. First, there has been the theme of trade unionism in British law. This was an especially controversial issue in the period before the outbreak of the First World War. Initially unions were declared liable for damages sustained during strikes, and then they were declared immune. Over the same period trade unionists were forbidden and then authorised to make contributions – by way of a 'political levy' – to a political party. In short, these were years of conflict and strife, all the more so because a sequence of extensive and sometimes violent strikes took place between 1908 and 1914. This important and controversial period in trade union history is analysed in Chapter 2.

The war years, 1914–18, witnessed a lessening of strike activity and an increase of national solidarity in the face of the common enemy. This period has been little studied. Most historians have chosen instead to focus their attention on the inter-war period and in particular on the General Strike of 1926. This is possibly the most important single event of the inter-war years; it is certainly one that has aroused considerable debate among historians. Three issues are considered in some depth in Chapter 5: the causes of the strike, the course of the nine-day conflict and why it lasted so short a time, and the consequences of the strike, including the 1927 Trade Disputes Act which re-opened the contentious issue of the position of the unions in law. Writers with a left-wing viewpoint have tended to blame the capitalists and to some extent the government for the strike, while those with the opposite political views have tended to blame the union leaders. The issue is a contentious one, and we must all make up our own minds about it. However, it should be remembered that other developments besides the General Strike took place between the wars. In particular the trade union movement, under the direction of men such as Ernest Bevin, made a substantial recovery in the late 1930s, moving closer to the Labour Party and taking a greater interest in political affairs than ever before. A summary of the changes produced in the movement before 1939 is offered in Chapter 7.

b) Economic Issues

The most common economic theme that has been identified in the period from 1900 to 1939 is that of Britain's economic decline. Indeed it could be said that historians have been obsessed with this issue and have, as a result, exaggerated its importance. Certainly it seems to have led some historians to neglect areas of the economy that were prospering. This emphasis on the nation's decline may stem partly from the fact that in the period after 1960 British people became acutely conscious that their country was falling behind its main rivals and therefore wished to trace the historical roots of this phenomenon.

Nevertheless it is understandable that this theme has been identified. After all, while in 1850 Britain had scarcely any economic rivals, at the start of the war in 1914 the United States and, in some industries, Germany were producing more than Britain. Chapter 2 considers the importance of 1900–14 and addresses the issue of whether by 1914 steep economic decline was inevitable. Chapter 3 examines the effects of the war itself. Most controversial of all is British economic performance in the inter-war period, which has been attacked by some writers while being applauded by others. The economy in the 1920s has tended to be ignored, with historians focusing on the 'Great Depression' of 1929–33 and on the nature of the recovery that followed. After 60 years of investigation, no consensus on economic performance in the 1930s has emerged. Much has been written on the mass unemployment and poverty that existed, and indeed the 'Hungry Thirties' is the most common image people today have of this period. But 'revisionist' historians have insisted that the 1930s were a boom period for the economy, when millions of jobs were created and affluence dawned. British economic performance between the wars is analysed in Chapter 4, where it is shown that the period was essentially one of contrasts, marked by high regional unemployment – especially among those who had worked in the once prosperous 'staple' industries – but also by high productivity and by the creation of new industries.

A common delusion is that economic history is simply a matter of establishing statistics for output, prices and wages and so on – that it is essentially quantitative. As a result, it is sometimes thought that there is little scope for controversy or doubt or imagination – or indeed for interest! But such a view is entirely mistaken. Statistics are indeed important for economic history: they help us to express things with conciseness, and they can be vivid and even shocking. But they are not the be-all and end-all of economic history. Disraeli once said that there are three kinds of lies: 'lies, damned lies and [worst of all] statistics'. All too often statistics can be manipulated to prove whatever we want them to, and certainly they must be treated with extreme care. We really need to know how statistics were computed in the first place, how reliable they are and, above all, exactly what they tell us. Often economic history is highly controversial and its study involves the full range of historical skills – a calculator is useful, but critical intelligence is of far more value!

Another important economic theme from 1900 to 1939 is the growing involvement of governments in the economy. By the latter date politicians intervened far more in economic issues and *laissez-faire* was no longer their basic attitude. Indeed, by the end of the inter-war period politicians were being influenced by the interventionist views of John Maynard Keynes, who in earlier days had been an outspoken critic of the financial establishment. Nevertheless it is important to realise that government involvement in the economy did not grow steadily. The years of war and its aftermath (1914–20) saw far greater government direction of the economy than at any other period covered by this book. Did government intervention in the economy prove constructive and effective? This is a highly controversial issue. It is covered in Chapter 3, on the war, and more specifically in Chapter 6, on the role of governments in the inter-war years. Particularly important is the issue of how constructively politicians reacted to the Great Depression and whether more could and should have been done to provide work for the unemployed in the 1930s. Far from being an arid, purely 'factual' topic, this is a lively one which almost automatically reflects contemporary political views about the appropriate role of governments in economic life.

This book is written in the belief that the history of industrial relations and of economic issues is as interesting, varied and stimulating as any other form of history. It is certainly as testing to students. It is also as important in its historical effects. Some historians even speak of the economy as the 'infrastructure' which affects, if not determines, the whole of history. In reality all forms of history are complementary; each affects and is affected by the others (though this is not to say that all are equally important at all times, since 'circumstances alter cases'). Those who wish to see British industrial relations and economic history from 1900 to 1939 in a wider context of political, social and international issues are recommended to consult the other books in this series.

Working on 'Introduction'

Detailed notes on this chapter are not required. The chapter has two objectives. The first is to provide you with a brief working knowledge of the main developments of the nineteenth century in the realms of the economy and of industrial relations. Events in the period 1900–39 can often only be fully understood by reference to earlier developments. The second aim is to provide you with a brief 'mental map' of the rest of the book and to introduce you to themes which you will later study in detail. You may find it worthwhile to refer back to this chapter, or at least to the study-diagram, to see how subsequent chapters form part of the book as a whole.

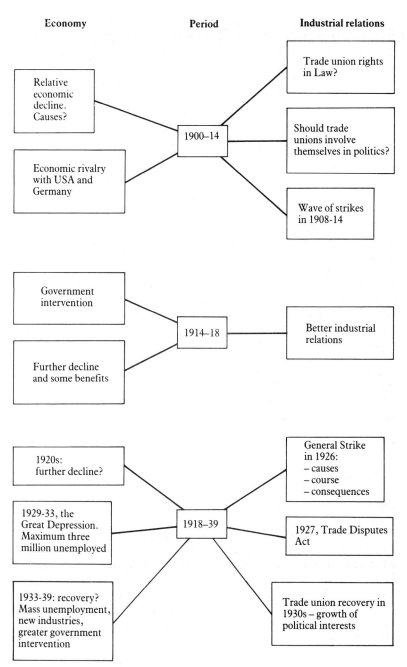

Economy	Period	Industrial relations

Relative economic decline. Causes?

Economic rivalry with USA and Germany

1900–14

Trade union rights in Law?

Should trade unions involve themselves in politics?

Wave of strikes in 1908-14

Government intervention

Further decline and some benefits

1914–18

Better industrial relations

1920s: further decline?

1929-33, the Great Depression. Maximum three million unemployed

1933-39: recovery? Mass unemployment, new industries, greater government intervention

1918–39

General Strike in 1926:
– causes
– course
– consequences

1927, Trade Disputes Act

Trade union recovery in 1930s – growth of political interests

Summary – Introduction

CHAPTER 2

1900–14: The Gathering Storm?

1 The British Economy in 1900

At the start of the twentieth century, Britain's economy was the most highly industrialised in the world. Its population, comprising only about two per cent of the world's total, was responsible for almost one-third of all trade in manufactured goods. Only the United States of America produced more goods than Britain, but per capita (that is, per head of population) Britain manufactured over 30 per cent more than the USA. In addition, Britain possessed the world's largest naval and merchant fleets, as well as the most extensive empire in history, covering about one-quarter of the world's land surface. This country invested far more capital abroad than any other, its currency (the pound sterling) was stronger than any other, and the City of London was the world's financial centre, acting as banker, money-lender and insurance broker on a vast scale.

The economy was strong and prosperous in 1900, remarkably so in view of Britain's tiny population and limited range of raw materials. Yet, although from our modern-day perspective we may be amazed at this economic success, there were many at the time who were dismayed at economic failure. They compared the position with the unrivalled supremacy enjoyed in the middle of the nineteenth century (see page 4). After all, only 20 years earlier Britain had been producing much more than the United States. Now, not only the USA but also Germany had overtaken British production of iron and steel.

British output was still increasing, but economic rivals were catching and even overtaking Britain. Many people became aware around 1900 that their country was experiencing an economic decline relative to its major competitors. Just before the start of the century a best-selling book, *Made in Germany*, had highlighted the degree to which German exports were penetrating the British market. Another volume, *American Invaders*, raised a similar warning about the United States. Now the difficulties Britain experienced in winning the Boer War (1899–1902) against Dutch settlers in South Africa seemed to underline British weakness. In Kipling's words, the British were given 'no end of a lesson'. It was popularly thought around this time that unless a country was growing ever stronger it would inevitably become weaker and decline. Was Britain therefore destined to follow the example of the Roman Empire, to decline and fall?

2 Economic Trends, 1900–14

a) The Views of Contemporaries

Many pessimistic commentators judged that Britain continued to decline after 1900. Germany was identified as the major threat. With its larger population (65 million compared with 45 million) and more abundant raw materials, Germany undoubtedly performed better economically, achieving a higher rate of growth. By 1913 it was responsible for a slightly higher percentage of world manufacturing output than Britain.

Yet if the fears of the pessimists seemed to be confirmed between 1900 and 1914, others were able to conclude that Britain was doing well and that the country had never been so prosperous. After all, Britain's output was increasing. Many took comfort from this fact and mocked those who harked back nostalgically to the 'good old days' of unrivalled British supremacy. For example, while 100 million tons of coal had been mined in 1870, when Britain stood supreme, output rose to 287 million tons in 1913, a greater total than in any previous year. Progress was unmistakable. Observers could point to important technological advances (such as the increasing use of electricity to drive spinning machines in the textile industry after 1905), to the high profits made by the 'staple' industries (see page 4), and to the growth of new industries like chemical engineering, cars, soap and confectionery. In particular, the economy seemed to boom between 1910 and 1913.

Contemporaries looked at Britain's economic performance in contrasting ways. This is not surprising: they were too close to events to achieve any real sense of perspective, and so their opinions could only be impressionistic. Indeed it was impossible for people in 1900–14 to judge the performance of the economy as a whole because reliable statistical evidence simply did not exist. National unemployment figures were not calculated, and nor was gross domestic product (GDP) – the sum value of all goods and services in the economy. Still less did they have authoritative evidence on Britain's past performance or on that of its foreign competitors.

b) The Period in Retrospect

Which group was correct, the optimists or the pessimists? This is a difficult question to answer because historians are also bedevilled by the lack of accurate statistics. However, most historians have judged that, because they are not mutually exclusive, both schools of thought were correct. There were positive and negative aspects to economic performance in these years.

By 1914 Britain still had a strong economy. It was easily the world's largest foreign investor, owning over 40 per cent of the world's foreign investment, a source of great wealth from dividends. Britain also owned most of the world's shipping and still produced a significant proportion of the world's manufactured goods – but it was a declining proportion. Economic historians argue about exact totals, but it seems likely that production of manufactured goods fell from around one-third of world output in 1900 to one-quarter in 1914. The economy was still growing, but the rate of growth was declining. Output was still rising after 1900 but not as quickly as previously. The American and the German economies were growing much more quickly – probably twice as fast – between 1900 and 1913.

It is also true that there were technological advances in Britain, but perhaps even more significant was the degree to which such change did not occur. This was particularly the case in the 'staple' industries. Despite the fact that some machines were powered by electricity, on the whole the textile industry failed to modernise. The same was true of the coal industry, where production rose but productivity (output per worker) fell. Output from British pits had never been higher than in 1913, but never before had so many miners been employed. Whereas coal mining in America and Germany was undergoing mechanisation, in Britain coal was still being extracted by old-fashioned methods, largely by men wielding picks. In fact, output per miner in Britain fell by around 20 per cent between 1880 and 1914, as men had to work on progressively thinner coal seams. By 1912 only one quarter of machines used in the mining and manufacturing industries were powered by electricity. Back in the middle of the nineteenth century Britain had spearheaded technological development, but this was no longer the case. Instead Britain was lagging behind its main competitors in this important area.

In other ways too the British economy was no longer progressive. It was the Americans, not the British, who introduced 'conveyor-belt' techniques of mass production, as in Henry Ford's car factories after 1900. The Americans also introduced a 'high wage' economy: workers were paid enough to buy the goods they produced, thus ensuring a high demand that stimulated production. In Britain, in contrast, there was a 'low wage' economy, so that only rich and middle-class people could afford to buy other than very simple manufactured goods. (Indeed the middle classes relied so much on cheap domestic servants that their need for labour-saving goods was small.) Thus the domestic market was very limited. Furthermore, it was the Americans and Germans who pioneered industry on a large scale, thus profiting from 'economies of scale' (the savings that can be made from bulk purchases and so on). In Britain factories were much smaller and so incurred relatively greater costs. Many industrialists in Britain were slow to adopt these new cost-cutting changes and also new and more efficient marketing and selling techniques.

Some new industries were appearing in Britain before 1914, and this was a promising sign. Yet the staple industries were still dominant in the economy, and since their products were meeting increasing competition from abroad they could not maintain their share of world trade. Exports of electrical goods, vehicles and aircraft – typical 'new' products – accounted for only 2.2 per cent of British exports by value in 1913. In contrast, cotton, woollens, coal, and iron and steel accounted for 51 per cent. In Germany and elsewhere governments provided subsidies to help new industries grow and flourish, but British governments did not. Because the industrial revolution had occurred 'from the bottom up' (as a result of the efforts of pioneering individuals rather than the actions of governments) people in Britain tended to place their trust in *laissez-faire*.

One positive aspect of the British economy was the financial expertise of the City of London. Its foreign investments and the financial services it offered to other nationals certainly produced high profits. Yet this should not disguise an important fact about the British economy in 1900–14. Britain was importing goods worth more than the goods it exported. The volume (and value) of British exports was growing, although more slowly than in earlier decades, but imports were growing even more rapidly. There was thus a deficit on the 'current account' – that is, the value of goods imported exceeded the value of goods exported. However, there was not an overall deficit, because on the 'capital account' so-called 'invisible exports' (profits from overseas investments and from financial transactions) more than compensated and so put the overall balance of payments in profit.

Overall, Britain was still an economically strong country in this period. It had in fact never been more prosperous. There was no decline in the sense of an absolute fall in production in 1900–14: indeed there was a very healthy absolute growth, averaging around two per cent a year. But the enormous lead over its rivals that had existed around the middle of the nineteenth century had been lost, and there had thus been a *relative* decline. Many historians see this as the most important theme of the period.

c) Britain's Relative Economic Decline

There has been an extensive debate among historians in recent decades about the causes of Britain's decline from being the 'workshop of the world' in the 1850s. So far there has been little agreement. This is perhaps not surprising. After all, Britain's relative decline was not an 'event', which might have a fairly simple explanation. Rather, it was a long and complex process, affecting some sectors of the economy and parts of the country much more than others. Nevertheless, it is generally agreed that collectively the following factors form the basis for a credible explanation.

i) Britain's economic supremacy in the mid-nineteenth century did not stem from an abundance of raw materials or the size of its population. Nor, as many fondly imagined at the time, was it due to the natural superiority of British people. It was simply 'a happy accident' (see page 4). It was therefore very unlikely to last long. It was not difficult for rivals to copy the industrial processes first begun in Britain. Indeed other countries, by starting the industrial race after Britain, could invest in the most modern equipment, while many British factories had to make do with relatively old-fashioned industrial plant. This interpretation is sometimes called the 'early start' thesis.

ii) Countries with more natural advantages than Britain were very likely, sooner or later, to overtake British production totals. Both the United States of America and Germany had larger populations and more abundant raw materials than Britain. When Britain had been experiencing its mid-nineteenth century industrial boom, these rivals had been unable to compete effectively. The United States was embroiled in civil war between 1861 and 1865, while Germany did not even become a unified state until 1871; but from the 1880s onwards, they were both in a good position to forge ahead more rapidly than Britain.

iii) Britain was handicapped by the trading policies of its rivals. Its economy had grown strong during the era of free trade. With no restrictions on trade, Britain had been able to buy in the cheapest market and sell in the dearest. Other countries found it hard to develop their own industries when British manufactured goods were usually so much cheaper and so much more reliable that they sold better than locally produced ones. But from the 1880s most trading nations imposed protective tariffs on incoming foreign goods: import duties raised the cost of foreign (including British) wares and so gave a fillip to local industries. Britain was alone amongst the leading trading nations in sticking to free trade.

iv) Perhaps too much capital went abroad. On average, between 1870 and 1914, 5.2 per cent of Britain's gross domestic product was invested abroad, and by 1914 £4,000 million was invested overseas. In some years more was invested abroad than at home, and indeed in 1911–13 twice as much went overseas. Perhaps this export of capital hindered domestic growth by starving British industry of finance; certainly it hastened the industrialisation of rivals.

v) Some historians have argued that a root cause of Britain's failure to maintain its industrial lead was the development of an 'anti-enterprise culture'. There is no doubt that the education system was very poorly geared to the needs of industry. It gave prominence to the classics (Latin and Greek) and to competitive sport, and there was not sufficient scientific research or technical education. In 1913 Germany produced six times as many science graduates as Britain. Perhaps the 'industrial spirit' never fully gripped the British people. Certainly trade and industry were often considered vulgar and socially demeaning.

Historians have often divided these causes of Britain's relative decline into the 'economic' and the 'social and psychological'. Another useful division is the 'avoidable' and the 'unavoidable'. Certainly some economic decline was inevitable. This word 'inevitable' should normally be avoided as people tend to use it when they mean only 'extremely likely'. However, its use is justifiable in this case because there was no chance that Britain could hold on indefinitely to the enormous lead which it had established in the middle of the nineteenth century due to special and short-lived circumstances. A measure of economic decline, in comparison with rivals such as the USA and Germany, was therefore inevitable. The key question was not whether Britain would decline, relative to its rivals, but how long and how steep this decline would be. Could the decline be halted or slowed down, or would it continue at an ever faster pace? Would British industry be technologically modernised? Would the old staple industries continue to dominate the British economy, or could other sectors produce new growth and productivity? Would 'invisible exports' continue to compensate for the imbalance between exports and imports?

A trend towards relative decline had been established by 1914, but the significance of that trend – how it would affect the future and form part of a larger pattern – was far from certain.

3 Trade Unions and the Law, 1900–14

The industrialisation of Britain in the nineteenth century produced not only great wealth but also exploitation and gross disparities of income. Trade unions had grown up to combat this inequality and to secure a better deal – essentially higher wages, but also improved conditions of work – for their members. By the end of the nineteenth century the unions had achieved recognition from the State (see page 7), but their exact position in law was still a matter for controversy among members of the judiciary.

In 1900 the unions, together with a number of small socialist societies, founded the Labour Representation Committee, which became known as the Labour Party from 1906. Many of the most radical union leaders wanted not merely to secure piecemeal improvements in particular industries but, in the words of one of them, 'to stamp out poverty from the land'. They realised that this necessitated political as well as economic action. Some other union leaders, wishing to stay out of politics, disapproved of this move: they were suspicious of ideas like 'socialism' and 'equality' and instead wished to maintain wage differentials between separate groups of workers. Yet, on the whole, the founding of the Labour Party seemed a sign that the trade unions were to become more influential than ever before. This proved to be the case, but only after challenges and setbacks.

a) The Taff Vale Case, 1900–2

Trade union success at the end of the nineteenth century, together with the growing confrontational atmosphere between employers and unions in the 1890s, provoked a backlash from those who felt that unions were becoming too powerful. In 1901 *The Times* argued that trade unions, by their restrictive practices, were responsible for Britain's weakening industrial position against foreign competition. A *Daily Mail* headline put it even more bluntly: 'American Furniture in England. A further indictment of the trade unions'. Some working men also disapproved of the new militant stand the unions were taking and formed the National Free Labour Association. This was essentially a team of men prepared to act as strike-breakers by taking over the work of men on strike. In 1900 members of the association were given contracts of employment by the Taff Vale railway company of South Wales, whose own employees were on strike. The local union fought back. Some strikers greased the railway track on inclines so that trains carrying 'blacklegs' could not reach their destination. Others organised picketing and tried to persuade the association members not to work. The company manager then took the issue to the courts, claiming damages from the union for inducement to breach of contract. The strike itself was soon over, but the legal case dragged on until 1902 when the House of Lords (the highest court in the land) ruled that the union would have to pay damages of £23,000 to the company, plus legal costs of £19,000.

This judgement was a severe blow to trade unionism. It has been called a 'judicial *coup d'état*' which made strikes 'for all practical purposes absolutely illegal'. It followed a legal ruling that seemed to forbid peaceful picketing and preceded by only a fortnight another which again awarded damages against a union involved in a strike. Henceforth unions were much more reluctant to call strikes since their funds might be confiscated in damages. Another result was that more trade unionists than before saw the need for a change in the law and therefore pinned their hopes on the Labour Party. However, the next setback seemed to cast doubts upon whether unions would even be allowed to support Labour.

b) The Osborne Judgement, 1909

A railway employee, Walter Osborne, a Liberal supporter, disliked the fact that a portion of his union fees went to help finance the Labour Party. Finding wealthy Liberal and Conservative backers, he took his case to the courts. At first he was unsuccessful, but eventually the House of Lords ruled in his favour, deciding that trade unions could no longer spend money for political purposes. The unions were now unable to support the Labour Party with donations from union fees, and nor could they pay the political expenses of Labour or trade union candidates in elections.

The Taff Vale ruling meant that the unions could not involve themselves in effective industrial action; the Osborne Judgement ruled out effective political action. There was in these years an effective anti-trade union lobby. Some feared – and others hoped – that British trade unions would decline in importance.

Yet by 1914 the unions were more powerful than ever. Their success was due in part to changes in Parliament arising from the elections of 1906 and 1910. In 1906 the Liberals achieved a great victory and, encouraged by Labour MPs, passed the 1906 Trade Disputes Act, which has been called 'the essential charter of trade unionism'. It legalised peaceful picketing and reversed the Taff Vale judgement, so that unions could no longer be sued for damages caused by strikes. The two elections of 1910 were much closer-run affairs. The Liberals were only kept in office by their allies, including Labour, and as a result Labour MPs were in a position to insist on further reforms favourable to the unions. In 1911 payment for MPs was agreed, each member of the House of Commons receiving a salary of £400 per annum. It was henceforth much easier for trade unionists and working men generally to become MPs. Then, in 1913, the Trade Union Act reversed the Osborne Judgement. Trade unions could now impose a 'political levy' on their members, providing that, in a ballot, over half the members of a union accepted the proposal and providing also that those who did not wish to pay the levy were given the opportunity to 'contract out' of doing so.

4 Waves of Industrial Unrest, 1908–14

a) What Happened

The years before the First World War saw not only an important strengthening of the unions' legal position but also a number of prolonged and bitter strikes. It was a period of unprecedented 'labour unrest'. Lenin, the Russian revolutionary, judged that British workers had embarked on 'the great heroic struggle for a new system of society'.

Between 1900 and 1907 there had been few major strikes in Britain. The average number of days lost in this period had been about 2.75 million per year. But in 1908 that figure jumped to almost 11 million, and in 1912 it reached a massive 41 million. In 1911 there were prolonged strikes by the dockers and seamen in support of a claim for higher wages. In Liverpool, where food supplies could pass through pickets only with a military escort, violence broke out. One policeman was killed and two men were shot by soldiers. The Lord Mayor of Liverpool feared that there would be a revolution, and warships were moored in the Mersey with their guns trained on the city. In the same year there was the first national strike on the railways in Britain's history. But perhaps the greatest trouble occurred in the mines.

A three-month strike took place in the Northumberland and Durham coalfields in 1910, to be followed shortly afterwards by a ten-month strike in South Wales, when the owners refused to give miners extra pay for working difficult seams. 'Blackleg' labour was used, and soon miners were fighting with police. Eventually cavalry was sent by the government to Tonypandy, where one miner was killed. In Llanelli two more were killed (one of whom was simply watching from his back garden as rioters threw stones at a train). Both these miners' strikes failed, but in March 1912 the Miners' Federation of Great Britain called a national strike to secure a minimum wage for all miners. One historian has called this strike 'the biggest stoppage the world had yet seen'. This time victory was achieved. The Coal Mines Act of 1912 established a system for setting minimum wages in the various coal mining districts. There was no single *national* minimum wage, but miners' leaders had achieved most of what they wanted and so recommended a return to work.

However, that was not an end to strikes or industrial violence. In the Dublin transport strike of 1913, clashes between police and strikers developed into riots in which hundreds were injured and two men died of fractured skulls. One historian has written that 'frightened police going berserk in baton charges were almost a commonplace' in the five years before the war.

b) Explanations

There are two main ways of explaining this wave of strikes. The first sees industrial activity as stemming from a new mood of political militancy among British workers and judges that, but for the outbreak of the First World War in 1914, workers might well have organised a general strike and perhaps even a revolution. The second considers the industrial disputes to be less significant in that they had basically economic origins and motivations which had largely run their course before the war began.

i) The Influence of Syndicalism

Many journalists were convinced that the wave of strikes was a portent of revolution. In 1911 Winston Churchill, the Home Secretary, said that Britain was about to be 'hurled into an abyss of horror', and the following year *The Times* judged the coal strike to be 'the greatest catastrophe that has threatened the country since the Spanish Armada'. Was this an over-reaction, or were the strikes indeed a sign of something more than economic discontent?

It has often been said that behind the workers' militancy lay the doctrine of syndicalism. This was a theory advocated by the French writer Georges Sorel. Like most socialists, Sorel believed that the interests of the owners of industry and of the workers were diametrically opposed. What distinguished his thinking was a new stress on the use of 'direct action' by workers to overthrow capitalism. He believed that workers in the same industry should be encouraged to join a single large union, so that strikes would be all the more complete and effective. In the end, such unions would cover every sector of industry. Strikes were to be used as a political weapon against the capitalists and, eventually, a general strike would take place which would overthrow capitalism altogether and lead to workers' control of industry.

The most important British convert to syndicalism was Tom Mann, one of the key figures in the history of British trade unionism. Already, in 1889, he had taken a leading role in the successful London dock strike (see page 6) when he had insisted that the true union policy should be one of aggression against the capitalists. Now, in 1910, he began to publish a radical monthly journal, the *Industrial Syndicalist*, and formed the National Transport Workers' Federation, very much the sort of large-scale union advocated by syndicalism. He also helped organise the dock strikes of the following year, urging strikers not to be 'too mealy-mouthed over law and order'.

There were others who were influenced by syndicalism as well. In South Wales during the disputes of 1912 a group of miners produced *The Miners' Next Step*, which clearly bore a syndicalist imprint:

1 Alliances [are] to be formed, and trades organisations fostered, with a view to steps being taken, to amalgamate all workers into one National and International union, to work for the taking over of all industries, by the workmen themselves . . .
5   The Irritation strike depends for its successful adoption, on the men holding clearly the point of view, that their interests and the employers [sic] are necessarily hostile. Further, that the employer is vulnerable only in one place, his profits! Therefore if the men wish to bring effective pressure to bear, they must use methods
10 which tend to reduce profits. One way of doing this is to decrease production, while continuing to work . . .
   Our objective begins to take shape before your eyes. Every industry thoroughly organised, in the first place, to gain control of, and then administer, that industry. The co-ordination of all
15 industries on a Central Production Board . . . who will issue its demands on the different departments of industry, leaving the men themselves to determine under what conditions and how, the work shall be done. This would mean real democracy in real life, making for real manhood and womanhood. Any other form of
20 democracy is a delusion and a snare.

This document has been called 'the classic statement of British syndicalism'.

A further sign of syndicalist influence may have appeared in 1914. Already several groups of unions had amalgamated, and now the 'triple alliance' was formed out of three of the largest federations of workers – the miners, the railwaymen and the transport workers. The power of these workers seemed such that they might use their combined industrial muscle to extract any concessions from their employers. Some have argued that the alliance's intention to launch a general strike on Britain was only averted by the outbreak of the First World War.

ii) Economic Causes of Unrest

Debate among the experts is continuing, but probably most historians now think that the influence of syndicalism on British industrial unrest was exaggerated by the press. It has been pointed out that, although some individuals like Tom Mann and the South Wales miners were clearly influenced by syndicalism, many more were not. According to this interpretation, the wave of strikes after 1908 can be satisfactorily explained partly by political circumstances, but primarily by economic factors.

In the few years before 1906 there were relatively few strikes in Britain. This was mainly due to the Taff Vale ruling, which made union leaders cautious about taking industrial action. After 1906 and the Trade Disputes Act there were likely to be more strikes – especially since economic grievances were beginning to multiply. In the final decades of the previous century prices had been falling, and therefore as long as union leaders could maintain wages at their existing levels their members had been better off. But now prices began to rise. This inflation put a great strain on industrial relations. Union leaders would have to secure pay rises simply in order for the standard of living of their men to remain stationary. Rising prices are seen by several historians as the key to the wave of strikes; and it follows from this that trade unionists, far from wanting to overthrow capitalism, merely wished to prevent a deterioration in the living standards of their members. Their actions, which some have called 'the great offensive', were primarily defensive. In fact only in 1914, after many strikes, did average real wages return to their 1909 level. Economic statistics indicate that real income in Britain grew by only 0.4 per cent a year in 1900–13, compared with 1.2 per cent in the 1890s and 3.5 per cent in the 1880s.

The economy is also said to explain another factor that helped produce strikes. Despite inflation, trade began to improve and the economy to expand after 1908. In particular the years 1911–13 have been called the 'great boom'. More people were employed, and in this situation not only did greater numbers join trade unions – so that total union membership grew from 2.4 million in 1910 to 4.1 million in 1913

– but there were fewer unemployed people to act as strike-breakers. Unions are always at an advantage when the 'trade cycle' (see page 48) is improving. Profits are then higher, and employers can generally afford to pay their workers better wages.

Furthermore there were special circumstances that explain particular disputes. In the coal industry, for instance, owners were reluctant to give higher wages because of the extra costs produced by government legislation, which now insisted on new safety regulations and on a maximum working day of eight hours. On the railways, where costs were rising, the government had pegged freight rates by an Act of Parliament. The result was that higher costs could not be reflected in higher prices, and so the firms reacted by introducing larger engines and rolling stock. As a result, many men found themselves shovelling twice as much coal for no increase in wages – a sure recipe for industrial friction.

5 Conclusion: a Gathering Storm?

a) Strikes

The years before the First World War certainly constituted a menacing period industrially. There was a definite militancy among many British workers. Union leaders seemed too moderate to some workers. Indeed it was said by the government's industrial relations expert, Sir George Askwith, that 'often there was more difference between the men and their leaders than between the latter and the employers.' It was thus, to some extent, a three-cornered contest: men *versus* unions *versus* employers. Owing partly to the growing size of many unions, a gulf began to open up between ordinary workers and their national leaders, several of whom had also become Members of Parliament. The result was that shop-floor grievances led to 'unofficial' strikes (that is, those not supported and organised by the unions). Small wonder that even Conservative politicians wished to see a stronger trade union movement: it was thought that unions, if well organised and disciplined, would lessen the influence of the militants and so reduce the number of strikes.

Militancy undoubtedly existed, but it did not necessarily constitute a real challenge to the government of the day. There is still room for doubt about the causes of the strikes of the period, especially since so little is known of many of them, but on balance it seems that a stronger case can be made out for the wave of strikes having primarily economic rather than political or syndicalist origins. Admittedly there was an unusual amount of violence in the strikes of 1910–12, but this may well have been due to government tactics. On several occasions the Home Secretary waived the normal rules and sent troops to disputes when the local authorities had not requested assistance. We should also bear in mind that some strikes were due to the intransigence of employers – many of whom wished to crush the unions – and to the lack of any widely accepted procedures for settling disputes between 'capital' and 'labour', factors that are too often ignored.

There is no single cause responsible for the increased strike activity that preceded the First World War. Economic factors are certainly vital, and yet they probably do not provide a complete explanation, especially for the new degree of working-class solidarity which many observers sensed. The government's expert, Sir George Askwith, pointed in a speech in 1913 to a number of causes of industrial strife:

1 There is a spirit abroad of unrest, of movement, a spirit and a desire of improvement, of alteration. We are in, perhaps, as quick an age of transition as there has been for many generations past. The causes of this are manifold. I am only going to indicate a few.

5 One is that the schoolmaster has been abroad in the land, and that, as education improves, the more a man wishes to get to a better and higher position . . . Again, every man, whatever the actual cost of his livelihood may be, if he has arrived at a particular standard of life, not only desires to improve it, but also

10 would struggle hard before he would give it up. When you come to certain standards of wages and livelihood, and find that particular things that you particularly use rise greatly in price, it affects the amenities of life and the margin of life to such an extent that there is disenchantment and a desire to keep to the standard

15 which may have been achieved. Then there is the spirit of movement throughout the world. We quicken day by day means of transport . . .

In addition to that you have in this country for some years past what I may call political equality. One man's vote is as good as

20 another – sometimes better. If a man has got educated up to the view of considering himself politically equal to another man, he is far more anxious to achieve a greater amount of economic equality; a desire to reach that economic equality must necessarily exist in his mind . . . That, shortly, sums up some of the reasons

25 why there is unrest, unrest that nobody can be surprised at, and which is bound to continue. Are men to remain in a backwater and do nothing . . . ?

What of the general strike that some insist would have occurred in 1914? It seems to have been only a bare possibility. Rather than strikes approaching a climax in the summer of 1914, there was a calming of the situation in 1913 and the first six months of 1914. Almost 41 million working days were lost in 1912, but in 1913 the total fell to just under ten million, with virtually the same figure for 1914. Significantly, *The*

Miners' Next Step was issued when militancy had already reached its height. It did not inspire further industrial action. In fact, as the syndicalist influence became more pronounced in South Wales, union membership there fell off, against the national trend. It has been said that a recession was on the way in the summer of 1914 and that, but for the war, the workers would have started a 'fresh wave of massive strikes' to protect the gains won in 1910–13. However, a general strike was very far from certain.

The 'triple alliance' was formed in the spring of 1914 not to spearhead a general strike but to avoid the need for strikes. The terms of the alliance did not allow its leaders simply to call a strike: instead union members had to be consulted, and in some cases balloted – a lengthy and complicated procedure. Ballots would have to be arranged not just for the 'federations' but for the numerous individual unions that comprised them. The president of the Railwaymen's union judged that the alliance 'is neither revolutionary nor Syndicalist. It is a force which is not intended to be used indiscriminately or frivolously'. One expert has commented that 'The attraction of the alliance . . . lay in the promise of bloodless battles'. In short, the leaders of the alliance probably hoped to achieve their objectives by bluff alone. Union leaders were prepared to use syndicalist slogans ('direct action', 'the general strike', 'workers' control of industry'), but syndicalism was not a dominant strand in union thinking.

Several writers have painted a picture of a nation ripe for revolution in 1914, one cataclysm only averted by an alternative cataclysm, the First World War. They have argued that not only industrial relations but the troubles in Ireland and the activities of the suffragettes pointed to violent revolution. 'Liberal England' was dying: instead of solving problems by discussion and reason, people were taking direct action. But the main problem with this view is that no one has managed to show convincingly that connections existed between these three separate, and in many ways dissimilar, problems. Of course it is impossible to *prove* that a civil war or revolution might not have occurred but for the start of the war. We can never be entirely certain about such hypothetical arguments. But the onus must surely be on those who seek to show that revolution was brewing to demonstrate their case convincingly. So far they have not done so.

Was there a 'gathering storm' in industrial relations from 1908 to 1914? There were industrial problems in plenty, and the strikes in 1910–12 must be considered industrial storms of the first magnitude. But those who employ this phrase about 1908–14 (or 1910–14) are implying that the squalls before 1914 were merely a prelude to a much larger storm, that the storm clouds were gathering for an almighty downpour. However, it seems that the worst was over by 1914. Certainly the press thought so, and the government needed to intervene less in industrial disputes after 1912. The clouds had not been dispelled, but the forecast was for showers or drizzle rather than storms.

b) The Economy

If industrial relations were not predestined to produce catastrophe by 1914, what of the economy as a whole? Was Britain heading downhill at breakneck speed? Were the clouds gathering for an economic storm?

Economic commentators at the time were sharply divided on this issue. While articles in *The Times* spoke of a 'crisis of industry' and pessimists predicted calamity, others looked forward to steady progress and increasing prosperity. Historians have tended to mirror this dichotomy of views.

Some writers have stressed the negative features of these years, and in particular the fact that Britain was declining relative to its major competitors. It had been overtaken by the United States during the 1890s, and now Germany was beginning to forge ahead. There were certainly problems for the British economy. Almost everywhere, including in its own domestic market, British goods faced intense competition, and often foreign markets were defended by protective tariffs. New manufactured goods were being produced, but their value was small in comparison with the economy as a whole, and Britain's exports relied overmuch on staple industries which were not being modernised and whose products were able to command only a diminishing share of world trade. Indeed, perhaps the most worrying of all Britain's failures was its inability to remain at the forefront of technological innovation. Britain had developed every major new technique in steel manufacture in the nineteenth century, and yet failed to apply most of them to its own steel industry. (For instance, the techniques pioneered by Sidney Gilchrist-Thomas in 1877–8 helped the French and Germans far more than his countrymen.) Britain's steel and railway industries in the 1900s have been called outdated 'industrial dinosaurs'. One historian has judged that, because of its failure to modernise, the world's 'leading and most dynamic economy' was quickly being transformed into 'the most sluggish and conservative'. The implication of this view is that decline was so precipitous that it could not be halted.

Yet more optimistic historians counter that it was only to be expected that Britain would be overtaken by two larger and naturally richer states, the USA and Germany. The far more significant issue was whether Britain would be overtaken by countries with similar resources and population size, such as France, and by 1914 there were few signs that this was likely to happen. The French achieved only a marginally higher rate of manufacturing growth than Britain between 1900 and 1913. If such a rate continued in the future, Britain would still be economically the much stronger power for generations to come. Admittedly there were problems for the economy, but these did not seem insuperable. Of Britain's exports, 35 per cent went to Europe, despite tariffs. Although Britain's share of world trade was diminishing, world trade was expanding very rapidly, and so in absolute terms British goods were selling in greater quantities than ever before. The staple industries were still making very healthy profits. 'New industries' may have accounted for only a relatively small share of the total economy, but there was no reason to suppose that they would not grow in the future. And, despite balance of trade problems, 'invisible exports' were remarkably lucrative. It has been argued that there were good reasons to believe that Britain was adjusting successfully to new international market forces.

Clearly the economic record before the war was mixed. Therefore it would be unwise to take an extreme 'optimistic' or 'pessimistic' viewpoint about Britain's future economic prospects. Britain was facing severe economic problems, but the country was still prosperous and there were numerous signs of material improvement for the British people. Would the new climate of international economic competition have an ultimately bracing or depressing effect on Britain? This was the key question, and it was one that could only be decided by future developments. A trend towards relative decline had certainly been established by 1914, but the significance of this trend would depend on Britain's economic performance over a much longer period. After all, trends do not carry on indefinitely: sometimes they are replaced by contrary trends. The longer-term future had not been predetermined by these years. There were economic problems ahead, but there was surely no 'gathering storm' in the sense that an inevitable economic catastrophe was brewing. Only the future could decide whether or when Britain's relative decline would end.

Perhaps the most important clouds on the horizon in 1908–14 stemmed from the menacing international situation. For years crises between the Great Powers in Europe had been threatening to unleash war. Britain's economy was, more than any other country's, integrated with that of the world. Britain traded more – and earned more from world commerce, both 'visible' and 'invisible' – than any other country. It also relied on an exceptionally high level of imports: over 50 per cent of food consumed in Britain was imported, as well as over 50 per cent of the raw materials used by industry. In a sense therefore, Britain, the world's largest creditor nation (lending more money than any other country), was also a dependent nation. It had far more to lose from war, and especially such a war as the Great War turned out to be.

Making notes on '1900–14: The Gathering Storm?'

You need to make fairly full notes on this chapter, especially since the

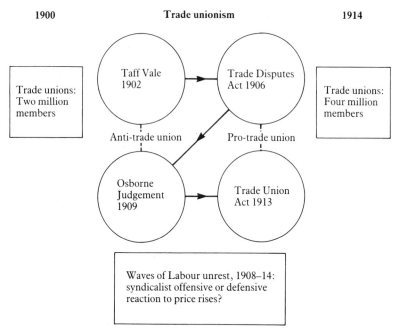

Summary – 1900–14: The Gathering Storm?

trends of the period 1900–14 were important for the issues covered later in this book. The headings and sub-headings in the text should help you to organise the material. Make a conscious effort to distinguish between 'facts' and 'interpretations' in your notes.

With factual material, especially statistics, remember that you do not need to copy down information in its entirety: instead you should express evidence in a form which *you* will be able to remember. At its most basic, this can mean that you note down mere trends, e.g. whether production was increasing or decreasing. Or you can express a percentage in approximate terms: 2.2 per cent can be rendered as 'just over two per cent', 23 per cent can be termed 'almost a quarter', and so on. There is no golden rule, except perhaps that you should tailor your notes to suit yourself.

As for interpretations, the most important thing initially is to grasp the essential ideas rather than the details. The first thing to do is to write down a very brief summary (normally no more than one sentence) of the interpretation in your own words. Then you may add extra details and illustrations if you wish to.

The final section of your notes (the conclusion) is one you could

Britain's economy

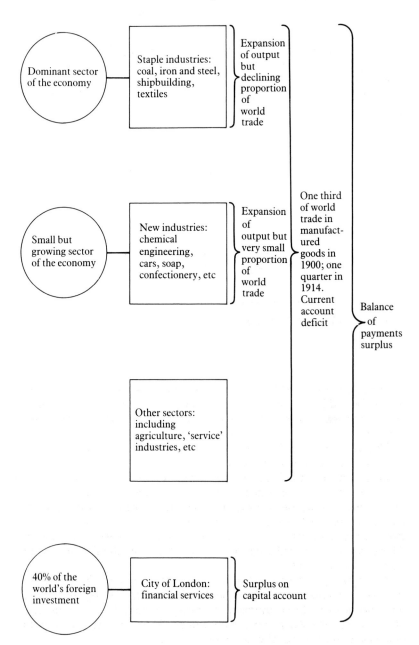

Summary – 1900-14: The Gathering Storm?

usefully make longer rather than shorter. Here you are dealing with overall judgements about the years 1900–14, and you should attempt to formulate your own verdicts. Hence, instead of simply making notes about what you have read, you should think for yourself, especially on the two key issues: first, industrial relations up to 1914 – how the strikes before 1914 are best explained and whether there was a 'gathering storm', and second, the performance of the British economy, and the significance of Britain's relative industrial decline.

One final suggestion: you may already have found yourself picking out certain 'technical' terms and making a note of what they mean. If you have not, it might be a good idea to do so. Keep this personal glossary (a collection of definitions) separate from your other notes. Such terms as 'relative decline', 'real wages', 'productivity' and others might be included at this stage. Add to your list as you read succeeding chapters.

Answering essay questions on '1900–14: The Gathering Storm?'

Many essay questions cover a wider period than 1900–14, but it is worth considering two on these years alone:

1   Why was there so much industrial unrest in the period 1900–14?
2   To what extent was the period between 1900 and 1914 one of steep economic decline for Great Britain?

The golden rule for writing history essays is simple – it is to 'answer the question, the whole question and nothing but the question'. No marks can be awarded for irrelevant material. The key to a good essay is often the first paragraph: in this you should establish the precise meaning of the question (including its component terms) as well as breaking it down into smaller, more manageable issues, each of which you will later develop into a whole paragraph. You can also outline your basic argument. Detailed advice on planning opening paragraphs is given in a companion volume to this one, *Britain: Domestic Politics, 1918–39*. See especially pages 36–37.

Attempt a first paragraph for each of the two questions above. Why do you think the wording of the second question stresses decline 'for' – rather than 'in' – Britain? How will you define 'steep' in this question?

Another vital part of the essay – indeed its culmination – is the final paragraph. In this you should be attempting to do several things:

i)   Having dealt with discrete aspects of the question in the middle paragraphs, you should now be recapping, drawing together the threads of your argument, and so returning to the whole question.

ii) You should be commenting on the various interpretations or 'schools of thought' relevant to the issue in the title and you should be giving your opinion on the central issue in the question set. Do not be afraid of giving *your* view: after all, this is what the question asks for. On the other hand, there is no need to use the words 'in my opinion' since your view should stem from the evidence you have brought forward. A merely personal view will not sound authoritative.

iii) Above all, you must hammer home your *conclusion*. So refer back to the original question and answer it as succinctly and clearly as you can. That does not mean that you have to be one-sided or audacious and shocking: you can be as judicious and cautious as you like. But whatever view you put forward, it must be clearly and forcefully expressed. Faint heart never won fair mark! In a conclusion, you must be conclusive.

Another way of considering this key area is to be aware of what you should *not* do. Do not load the paragraph down with factual information. Instead, you should be drawing logical conclusions from the facts brought forward in earlier paragraphs. Do not merely repeat what you have said already in the essay. And do not spring some new and unexpected idea that you have just thought of on the reader: more often than not, this will contradict views expressed earlier in the essay. The conclusion should stem logically from the rest of the essay. Nor should you 'look forward' and introduce another topic. For instance, you should not, having looked at 1900–14, then go on to write a brief introduction to 1914–18. Such irrelevancy – while common enough amongst examinees – actually loses marks rather than scores them.

You might practise writing brief conclusions, say six to eight lines, for both of the above essay titles. Take your time over this and do not be satisfied until you are sure your mini-conclusion cannot be improved upon. (It may seem paradoxical or even perverse to start at the end, but this is not a bad way of beginning preparation for writing an essay. It will prevent inconsistency, and in addition it should ensure that the essay is leading somewhere.)

Source-based questions on '1900–14: The Gathering Storm?'

1 *The Miners' Next Step*
Read the extracts on page 21 and answer the following questions:
a) What aspects of the programme could be called 'syndicalist'? Explain your answer. (*5 marks*)
b) What is missing from the full syndicalist programme? (*3 marks*)

c) Explain how, in the authors' opinion, the 'irritation strike' would further the cause of the workers. *(2 marks)*

d) In what sense would the programme produce 'real democracy'? In what ways do you think it might be undemocratic? *(5 marks)*

2 Sir George Askwith's view of strikes

Read the extracts from Askwith's speech on page 24 and answer the following questions:

a) What do you think Askwith meant by an 'age of transition' (line 3)? *(2 marks)*

b) Explain his references to the influence of i) 'the schoolmaster' (line 4), and ii) 'means of transport' (line 16). *(4 marks)*

c) Is he saying, on balance, that strikers wanted to improve or merely to protect their standard of living? Explain your answer. *(4 marks)*

d) By references to the text, explain whether Askwith approved or disapproved of strikes. *(4 marks)*

e) Can this speech be used as evidence of anything more than one person's views? Explain your answer. *(6 marks)*

CHAPTER 3

The First World War

The outbreak of war in August 1914 produced immediate changes in industrial relations. Some socialists, hoping that the British would refuse to fight against their fellow workers from Germany, called for a general strike. A left-wing paper insisted that only the class war was worth waging and that the workers had no country. Were not all workers, of whatever nationality, members of the same exploited class? Were they not, in fact, all brothers? The answer forthcoming was in the negative, as men flocked to enlist. If civil war was a possibility in July 1914, revolution was quickly forgotten in August. The common German enemy boosted national unity in Britain.

The government assumed that the war would be won by Christmas. This was a great error, for the destructive power of modern weaponry ruled out an early victory for either side. Technological advance in the nineteenth century had produced weapons of tremendous destructive power – not only reliable and accurate long-range rifles but also machine guns, able to fire 50 bullets a second. These new weapons, while too bulky to be easily carried, were especially powerful in defence, and the First World War therefore turned out to be a conflict in which defensive forces played a central role. The bulk of the fighting took place in France, on the western front: troops dug themselves in, and though both sides made periodic attacks, very little territory could be taken. After November 1914 the 'front line' was not to move by ten miles in any direction for the next three years.

The armies of Europe had an insatiable demand for munitions. As a result, this was a war not just between armies but between economies: it was a producers' war and an engineers' war. The 'front line' depended on the 'home front'. Britain's economy had to be put on a war footing. Never before had Britain's economic performance been of such momentous significance. Good industrial relations also mattered more than ever before. Strikes in British industry could literally be a matter of life and death for those fighting in France.

War has been called the 'locomotive of history'. Certainly the war was the major factor producing change in Britain between 1914 and 1918. The war tested all aspects of the British economy to the full – not only its industrial production but also its agriculture, its trade and its finance.

1 The Wartime Economy

At first it was assumed that private enterprise would supply the materials needed for the successful prosecution of the war, but soon politicians saw the necessity for government intervention to maximise production.

The war produced political turmoil. In 1915 Prime Minister Asquith formed a coalition government, and the following year he was replaced as premier by Lloyd George, who gave new impetus to the direction of the war. Lloyd George's methods were not orthodox, but he did manage to get things done. A contemporary summed him up: the new Prime Minister 'cares nothing for precedents and knows no principles, but he has fire in his belly, and that is what we want'. Before the war he had been the Liberal least committed to *laissez-faire*, and now he ended it completely. He believed that war was too serious a business to be left to free market forces.

At the start of the war the government, realising the vital importance of transport in modern warfare, took control of Britain's railway system. The following year a Ministry of Munitions was created: for the first time the State manufactured arms and ammunition. Although this ministry may not have been run with quite the efficiency and precision that Lloyd George, its first minister, later implied in his memoirs, it did open 60 new armaments factories by the end of 1915, and by the end of the war it had over three million workers under its direction. One control seemed to lead to another, as the government sought to increase Britain's economic efficiency in this increasingly desperate and destructive war. Control of shipping and the mines was added to the railways, and soon the government had banned strikes, rationed food and introduced conscription to the army. By the summer of 1918 the government virtually controlled the whole of British industry, as well as importing 90 per cent of goods that entered the country and marketing 80 per cent of the food consumed at home. Mistakes were undoubtedly made, but on the whole British resources were effectively mobilised to aid the war effort. Just over 60 per cent of the entire work force became directly engaged in war work.

The government had the difficult task of providing troops for the army while at the same time maintaining a large enough work force to produce the war material that was required. The army expanded rapidly. By the end of 1914 over one million men had volunteered, far more than had been expected. As a result, many had no weapons and drilled with wooden rifles. By the end of 1915 there were two and a half million in the armed forces, including many skilled craftsmen who could not really be spared from industry. In 1916 therefore a form of military conscription was introduced which enabled the army to expand while retaining key workers for the home front. This system was intensified the following year, and in the spring of 1918 conscription was extended to include men up to the age of 50. In the final year of war, despite heavy casualties, there were about four million men in the armed forces. A massive 46 per cent of all workers were then in the army.

We have to ask, in the light of this enormous military expansion, how Britain's industry was manned. Perhaps we should say 'personnel', for of the two and a half million extra people who entered the work force, most were women entering paid employment for the first time. About 750,000 women took jobs in manufacturing, and especially munitions production, while almost the same number took on clerical, transport and other work. The number of paid women workers grew by 50 per cent during the war, constituting a highly significant change in employment patterns and in the position of women in British society. A blow was being dealt to the Victorian beliefs that a woman's place was in the home and that women's work outside the home should be restricted to traditional 'caring' roles. The remaining million extra workers were men who put off retirement or who had previously been unemployed. The result was a gratifying one for the government: the size of the domestic work force declined by only about one million, despite massive recruitment to the army. A reasonable balance had been struck between the needs of the army and the requirements of industry.

Statistics illustrate the gigantic war effort of the British. 187 million shells were manufactured and sent to France; and whereas in 1914 274 machine guns were made, in 1918 total output was over 120,000. In addition, clothing and footwear for the troops were produced on a vast scale. For example, 45 million pairs of boots and 33 million jackets were sent to the front.

In addition, the government had other and scarcely less important concerns. How was the vast wartime effort to be paid for? Money as well as manpower was vital. The cost of the war in monetary terms was enormous. In 1913 the government had spent just under £200 million, slightly less than it raised in taxation. The budget was therefore balanced. But now the government had to spend more than ever before. By 1917 £7 million was being expended on the war every day. In 1918 the government spent a total of over £2,500 million while raising less than £900 million in taxation, thus creating a massive budget deficit.

During the war the British people were taxed much more highly than ever before. Indirect taxes (taxes on the purchase of goods) could not be raised by large amounts, since this would only cause inflation and fuel wage claims. But direct taxation was another matter, and the standard rate of tax was increased from about six per cent to 25 per cent, while over six million more people became eligible to pay it. Yet despite this, taxes paid for only about 30 per cent of the cost of the war (a relatively high proportion in international terms: the Germans raised only half this percentage from taxation). The rest of the money was raised by selling overseas assets (estimates of the proportion sold vary from 10 to 25 per cent of overseas investments), by the sale of government bonds to the public, and by borrowing from abroad, especially from the USA. At the end of the war Britain owed the

Americans about £1,000 million. Thus the true costs of the war had not yet been paid, and they would have to be borne by the post-war taxpayer.

The government also had to concern itself with other, more general, aspects of the economy, if only to ensure that the public's morale was high and that work was performed adequately. The submarine warfare in the Atlantic meant that imported goods, including food, were often in short supply, and so the government had to encourage the maximum production of home-grown food. It also had to take account of grievances over the cost of living. The war years were years of inflation. Food prices rose by ten per cent in the first month of war, and the cost of living index (a general guide to British prices) rose steadily thereafter (see the table below). Prices had roughly doubled by 1918. The key question was whether wages would keep pace with this inflation. Here was one significant problem for industrial relations, and there were others too. How would the trade unions react to the unprecedented changes of these years, and in particular to the admission of women to do 'men's work' in industry?

Wage and price levels		
	Prices	Wages
1914	100	100
1916	146	121
1918	203	195

2 Industrial Relations During the War

British trade unions reacted patriotically when the war began. The TUC called for an 'industrial truce' and urged that existing strikes be settled quickly. The number of working days lost in strikes in December 1914 totalled only three per cent of those lost in the last month of peace. Many unions even acted as recruiting agencies for the army. Union leaders recognised that the war could not be won unless their members rallied to the common cause, a fact of which the government was equally aware. There were therefore attempts to take the unions into partnership with government. It has been said that in 1914 British labour 'came of age' in that its position as a vital element in the economy was officially recognised. Labour and capital were seen to be equally important, and the government formed a 'triangular collaboration' with both. The aim was that government, businessmen and trade union leaders should co-operate wholeheartedly together.

Trade union leaders were given vital war work to do. Places were found in government for several of them, while the leader of the Labour Party, Arthur Henderson, soon became a member of the War Cabinet.

In 1915 Lloyd George hammered out an important agreement with the unions. In March he invited union leaders to a three-day conference at the Treasury. The Labour newspaper, the *Daily Herald*, commented with some trepidation that 'the trade union lamb had lain down with the capitalist lion'. The result was the 'Treasury Agreement', which specified that unions involved in vital war work would not strike: instead, if a compromise could not be reached by two sides in a dispute, an impartial tribunal would arrange arbitration. The unions also agreed to suspend traditional ('restrictive') working practices (such as specifying that only certain skilled men should undertake particular tasks) since these would tend to limit output. In return they were promised that the old arrangements would be resumed after the war and that the profits of firms benefiting from the agreement would be limited to 20 per cent above their 1914 levels. If profits exceeded this level, an excess profits tax of 100 per cent would be levied. This was only a voluntary agreement, but in July it was followed by the Munitions of War Act. This went further, in that it was legally binding, and although it only applied at first to munitions workers, it could be extended to cover any other group. The Act banned strikes by workers and 'lockouts' by employers, made the restriction of output an offence (so that normal working practices and hours of employment could be changed), and put some safety regulations into abeyance. It also became illegal for workers in key production posts to switch jobs without permission: they would first have to obtain a 'leaving certificate'. This procedure was designed to prevent the loss of valuable production and to stop employers 'poaching' skilled workers from one another.

Some workers objected to these arrangements. They believed that since trade unions were no longer putting pressure on employers for higher wages and better conditions of service, they were no longer fulfilling their proper functions. Complaints were especially voluble against union acceptance of 'dilution' in 1915. Many trade unionists in skilled and vital jobs had volunteered to join the army, and since skilled craftsmen were not available to take their places, and it would take too long to train apprentices, trade union leaders accepted that it was necessary to replace them with unskilled workers, including women. Thus the job of the skilled worker was 'diluted' by being broken up into a series of simpler tasks which the unskilled could perform. Union officials even supervised the process of dilution and made sure it worked effectively. In this way, the unions were contributing significantly to the war effort. But to critics, such wartime changes were unacceptable: the unions seemed not so much partners with the government, as their agents or even their lackeys.

How should the unions react to the war? Lloyd George had no doubt where their duty lay. While British soldiers were giving their lives, British workers had a duty to rally to the cause. In a speech in February 1915 he said:

1 Much as I should like to talk about the need for more men, that is
not the point of my special appeal today. We stand more in need
of equipment than we do of men. This is an engineers' war, and it
will be won or lost owing to the efforts or shortcomings of
5 engineers . . . We need men, but we need arms more than men,
and delay in producing them is full of peril for this country . . .
There are all sorts of regulations for restricting output. There are
reasons why they have been built up . . . The workmen had to
fight for them for their own protection, but in a period of war
10 there is a suspension of ordinary law. Output is everything in this
war.

    Most of our workmen are putting every ounce of strength into
this urgent work for their country, loyally and patriotically. But
that is not true of all. There are some, I am sorry to say, who shirk
15 their duty in this great emergency. I hear of workmen in
armaments works who refuse to work a full week's work for the
nation's need . . . They are a minority. The vast majority belong
to a class we can depend upon. The others are in a minority. But,
you must remember, a small minority of workmen can throw a
20 whole works out of gear. What is the reason? Sometimes it is one
thing, sometimes it is another, but let us be perfectly candid. It is
mostly the lure of the drink . . . Drink is doing us more damage in
the war than all the German submarines put together.

Many workers saw the need to accept sacrifices for the common
effort. Yet there were alternative voices. One was that of a miners'
leader, A.J. Cook, who had been an effective Baptist preacher in his
earlier years and who had been much influenced by syndicalism. In
April 1916 he urged miners to oppose collaboration with the capitalist
enemy:

1 Daily I see signs amongst the working class with whom I move
and work of a mighty awakening. The chloroforming pill of
patriotism is failing in its power to drug the mind and consciousness of the worker. He is beginning to shudder at his stupidity in
5 allowing himself to become a party to such a catastrophe as we see
today. The chains of slavery are being welded tighter upon us
than ever. The ruling classes are over-reaching themselves in their
hurry to enslave us . . . Economic conditions are forcing the
workers to think; the scales are falling from their eyes. Men are
10 wanted to give a lead. Comrades, I appeal to you to rouse your
union to protect the liberties of its members. An industrial truce
was entered into by our leaders behind our backs which has
opened the way for any encroachment upon our rights and
liberties. Away with the industrial truce! We must not stand by

15 and allow the workers to be exploited and our liberties taken away.

Militant trade unionists were willing to challenge not only the government but also their own moderate leaders during the war. The unions were in a very strong position because there was full employment. Union membership increased from about four million at the start of the war to six million at its close. Trade union leaders could have used this strength to extract concessions from employers and the government, but instead they accepted the need for sacrifice. Yet could they take their membership with them? As the war dragged on and as the cost of living rose, a great strain was put on their loyalty.

a) Industrial Strife

In many ways, trade unionists made important gains during the war. The fact that government controlled so much of industry led to national, as opposed to local, wage agreements. The miners finally achieved their aim of national wage rates. Furthermore, the length of the average working week fell from 55 to 45 hours. In some industries much better conditions of service came about. In the docks, for instance, the 'decasualisation' of labour began. Before the war, men were selected for employment on a daily basis, as ships needed to be loaded or unloaded, and so did not earn regular wages. But during the wartime shortage of labour, the dockers were given regular contracts of employment. A welfare department in the Ministry of Munitions also helped to bring about much improved conditions of work, so that almost 1,000 works canteens were built. It was coming to be realised that welfare was a vital factor in producing efficiency.

The main factor promoting tension was inflation. Wage rates rose during the war, so that by 1918 real wages stood, on average, only a few per cent below their 1914 levels (see the table on page 36). Indeed these wage rates do not take account of overtime payments, so that not all workers were marginally worse off by the end of the war and some were much better off. But even so an annual inflation rate of about 25 per cent undoubtedly exacerbated industrial tensions, and around the middle of the war wages seemed to lag significantly behind prices. In fact the First World War, which saw so much harmony in industrial relations, also saw significant strife.

Strikes had been outlawed in 1915, and over the next years the government set up machinery to arbitrate between workers and employers. It was arranged that in each industry there would be a joint council of employers and union representatives at national, district and works levels. But still strikes occurred. In fact only two weeks after industrial action was forbidden, 200,000 miners went on an unofficial strike in South Wales. It was impossible to arrest so many law-breakers, so the government put pressure on the mine owners to grant the men's demands for wage increases. The following year the government decided to take control of the mines itself in order to prevent further trouble.

The other main area of industrial conflict in the early years of the war was on Clydeside, in the shipyards of Glasgow. Here many craftsmen were angered by the acceptance of dilution by their union, the Amalgamated Society of Engineers, and their grievances were taken up by those who, before the war, had been influenced by syndicalism. The war had been a tremendous blow for those who wished to see working-class solidarity against the capitalist oppressors, but it was not a final defeat. Alternative leaders stepped in to perform the duties which the official union leaders now seemed unwilling to undertake. These were shop stewards, men appointed before the war to represent union members in individual workshops. Now they claimed to speak for all the men, of every union or of none. They were the most radical – and perhaps revolutionary – figures on the left during the war.

Glasgow's shop stewards opposed both the Treasury Agreement and the Munitions Act. They were not willing to suspend strike activity for the duration. They arranged several unofficial strikes in 1915, and when at the end of the year a victory was won – and steeply rising rents were pegged to their 1914 level – their prestige was high. They set up the Clyde Workers' Committee. Lloyd George himself decided to visit the Clyde to appeal for unity in December 1915. Everything was carefully stage-managed: there were workers in khaki uniform, a choir sang patriotic songs, the Union Jack was proudly displayed, and Labour's Arthur Henderson introduced him – but all to no avail. Disrespectful cries of 'Get your hair cut' rang out, and soon Lloyd George was shouted down. He was told that the Munitions Act 'has the taint of slavery about it'.

The shop stewards opposed dilution on the Clyde, but the government imposed it nevertheless, despite a series of strikes early in 1916. Seven shop stewards were arrested and imprisoned for sedition, while others were deported to other areas of Scotland. Government spokesmen claimed that a major attempt to sabotage the war effort had been averted. The movement had certainly been dealt a major blow. Defeat on the Clyde was followed by an attempt to create a nationwide shop stewards' movement, but without much success. Perhaps the shop stewards' fundamental weakness was that, whereas they themselves were radicals (and some even revolutionaries), their main support came from a group of very conservative craftsmen, whose central concern was to preserve traditional practices and their own high rates of pay. Such men were willing to fight a rearguard action to maintain their own privileges, but fundamentally there was little in common between their outlook and that of the shop stewards.

The Clyde was relatively quiet in 1917 and 1918, but not so British industry as a whole. In 1917, a rash of strikes threatened the whole war effort. Over 5.6 million working days were lost in 1917, and roughly the same number in 1918. In May 1917 there were engineers' strikes in Coventry, Manchester, Sheffield and elsewhere. An enquiry revealed many of the causes of the trouble. People were angry about high food prices, high rents and war profiteering. The excess profits tax was being widely avoided. There was also a high degree of overcrowding, as very few houses were built during the war, and conscription was proving very unpopular. It was also found that many workers believed that their trade union officials 'are no longer to be relied on'. There were, in fact, unmistakable signs that the population was war-weary, drawing from one historian the comment that 'civilian willpower was near to breaking point'. The government denounced the strikes as 'unpatriotic activity', and some ministers wished to declare martial law and conscript the strikers. But the Prime Minister decided that the only real answer was to grant pay rises to allow workers to return to their accustomed level of real wages. The government also abandoned the 'leaving certificate', which was proving unpopular.

The strikes were, on the whole, not a sign of revolutionary activity in British industry. Indeed one might be surprised that industrial unrest was not more pronounced towards the end of the war. Strikes arose mainly because the government could neither stop inflation nor devise a means of adjusting national wages in line with it. At the same time, calls for workers to show patriotism had begun to wear thin. Lloyd George commented in Cabinet that, at bottom, workers' grievances were 'genuine and legitimate', though adding that there was a real danger that these would be 'exploited by violent anarchists'.

Industrial unrest worried the government enormously in 1917 and 1918. The Bolshevik revolution in Russia seemed to give a fillip to revolutionary groups in Britain, and it was tempting to believe that deep-seated plots lay behind the wave of strikes of this period. There were rumours of a possible general strike, and a workers' soviet was set up in Glasgow, before its leader was sentenced to five years' imprisonment with hard labour. A.J. Cook was also prosecuted, in March 1918, for preaching revolution. Nevertheless, despite these fears and isolated incidents, enough was done by the end of the war to remove grievances and so to blunt the edge of militancy.

3 Conclusion: Effects of the War

a) The Economy

The war came to an end on 11 November 1918. It had produced major economic changes. Indeed it is no exaggeration to say that British industry had been transformed by the mobilisation of millions of soldiers and by an unprecedented switch to war production. The government had been forced to take control of the economy as never before, being criticised when things went badly and ultimately being praised when the war was won. Most historians agree that the history of the wartime economy was at least a partial success story: the economic price paid by Britain contributed, in the end, towards victory in the war.

Nevertheless the war posed major challenges to Britain's economic future. Massive amounts of money had been borrowed and would have to be repaid, while British loans to Russia were repudiated by the new Soviet government. In fact the National Debt had increased twelvefold by 1919. In addition, about 750,000 men had perished in the conflict (nine per cent of all men under 45 years of age), and twice that number had been very badly wounded. A productive section of the work force had been lost. So had valuable overseas markets. Could Britain win back its former customers? The war had produced a massive invest-ment in the staple industries, especially in iron and steel, coal and agriculture. But would such goods sell in vast quantities after the war?

Yet the economic effects of the war were not all bad. The British economy had shown a new productive capacity. One historian has commented that 'The stimulus of war ... infused a fresh spirit of enterprise into British industry'. Total output had fallen slightly, because of the smaller workforce, but productivity had definitely increased. There had been much state-sponsored modernisation, in-cluding a greater standardisation of engineering products. Electric power was used more than ever before, especially in the munitions factories, and the aircraft industry had developed significantly. The removal of so many skilled workers from industry, which had initially seemed to threaten economic collapse, had in fact stimulated much-needed mechanisation. The efficiency of agriculture had also increased, especially with the widespread introduction of the tractor.

The key question was whether the economy could switch efficiently to meet peacetime needs. And would there be a balance of trade after the war, or would imports exceed exports? Even before the war, Britain had imported goods of greater value than those it exported, and now that some overseas investments had been sold the so-called 'invisible exports' would not be so lucrative. There were likely to be major problems ahead for the British economy, but in the immediate aftermath of war no one could be certain whether the pre-war trend of relative British economic decline would gather pace or be reversed.

b) Industrial Relations

There were further unanswered questions in the field of industrial relations. Would the partnership between government and trade unions be maintained after the war? There had already been signs in 1917–18 that it was seriously under threat. Were the strikes of this period a sign of a fundamental antagonism between capital and labour that might even produce some sort of revolution? This was a real fear.

It was also uncertain whether official trade union leadership would be able to guide working-class discontent into constructive and constitutional channels or whether the shop stewards' movement or other radicals would take control. Would normal working practices be resumed, as the government had promised, or would employers seek to perpetuate wartime arrangements? If the latter, then the shop stewards might well find increasing support. If the former, how would women react on being forced to leave industry?

On average, by the end of the war rates of pay had virtually returned to their pre-war levels, in real terms. But there were significant variations between different groups of workers. On the whole, pay differentials had been eroded. Before the war, a skilled worker might well have earned three times as much as an unskilled colleague. Now this inequality had diminished, partly because wartime pay rises were often flat-rate increases (set amounts) rather than percentages and partly because unskilled workers were put on 'piecework', a system where pay depended on output. As a result, many unskilled workers, with overtime, were taking home much more money than ever before, some more than skilled workers. Would the craftsmen now attempt to return to their privileged position? And would workers as a whole, having shown restraint during the war, seek large increases now that the war was over? And what of those employees, such as teachers, whose pay had failed to keep up with price rises? Would they now take to strike action?

By the end of the war joint councils had been set up for several industries, composed of representatives of workers and employers. It was hoped that these would promote industrial peace by settling wages and conditions of service by negotiation and compromise. Could these herald for peacetime a new and more constructive method of settling industrial problems than the old way of confrontation and strikes? No one could yet be certain.

Peace came to Europe in November 1918. The fighting stopped immediately, but the consequences of war were to be long-lasting. Certainly there could be no resumption where the British economy and industrial relations had left off in 1914. The war had changed Britain irrevocably, and its effects would continue to be felt for the foreseeable future.

Making notes on 'The First World War'

You need to compile a detailed summary of the effects of the war on the British economy and on industrial relations. The headings and sub-

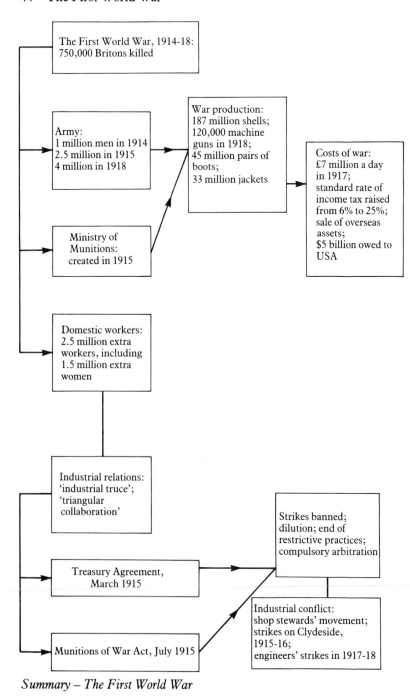

The First World War, 1914-18:
750,000 Britons killed

Army:
1 million men in 1914
2.5 million in 1915
4 million in 1918

Ministry of
Munitions:
created in 1915

War production:
187 million shells;
120,000 machine
guns in 1918;
45 million pairs of
boots;
33 million jackets

Costs of war:
£7 million a day
in 1917;
standard rate of
income tax raised
from 6% to 25%;
sale of overseas
assets;
$5 billion owed to
USA

Domestic workers:
2.5 million extra
workers, including
1.5 million extra
women

Industrial relations:
'industrial truce';
'triangular
collaboration'

Treasury Agreement,
March 1915

Munitions of War Act, July 1915

Strikes banned;
dilution; end of
restrictive practices;
compulsory arbitration

Industrial conflict:
shop stewards' movement;
strikes on Clydeside,
1915-16;
engineers' strikes in 1917-18

Summary – The First World War

headings used in the chapter should help you to organise the material efficiently.

As in the previous chapter, you should try to expand the final section ('Conclusion') by attempting to formulate your own judgements about the significance of the war years. As a means of doing this, you might briefly answer the following questions:

1   What were a) the successes, and b) the failures of the governments of the war years, in terms of both industrial relations and the economy? A four-box matrix might be the best way to lay out your answer to this question.
2   What changes took place in industrial relations between 1914 and 1918?
3   In what ways did the British economy a) gain, and b) lose from the First World War?

Answering essay questions on 'The First World War'

Questions can centre on industrial relations, either in 1914–18 or bracketed in a wider timescale. But perhaps the most popular question on the war years looks at the degree to which the war produced economic change in Britain. A typical title is:

To what extent did the First World War lead to economic change on the Home Front between 1914 and 1918?

It is worth spending some time trying to work out an overall argument in answer to this question. This might then form the basis of a final paragraph. How might you proceed? Think in terms of a) the degree of overall ('quantitative') economic change, and then b) the types of particular change ('qualitative'). Perhaps try a 'brain-storming' session. Which particular groups of workers might you focus on? Do you think it will be relevant to stress the degree to which Britain's international trading position was affected, or does the 'Home Front' preclude this aspect? Make sure that the form of words you choose answers the question directly: since it asks 'to what extent' you must conclude by specifying the extent as precisely as possible.

Source-based questions on 'The First World War'

1 Speeches by Lloyd George and A.J. Cook
Read the extracts from speeches by Lloyd George and A.J. Cook on pages 38 and 39. Answer the following questions:

a) With what justification did Lloyd George say that 'we need arms more than men' (page 38 line 4)? *(4 marks)*
b) How much appreciation did Lloyd George show of the difficulties faced by trade unionists and workers generally? Explain your answer. *(5 marks)*
c) What did Cook mean by 'the chloroforming pill of patriotism' (page 38 line 2)? *(2 marks)*
d) To what was Cook referring when he said that 'our rights and liberties' (page 38 line 12) were being encroached upon? *(3 marks)*
e) Which of the two speeches do you think would have had more appeal to British workers in 1915–16? Explain your answer. *(6 marks)*

CHAPTER 4

The Inter-war Years: an Economy in Decline?

How did the the British economy perform between 1918 and 1939? This seems like a straightforward question, involving 'fact' rather than 'interpretation'. It may be thought that statistics will provide an objective answer. Yet this issue has resulted in considerable controversy among the experts. The inter-war years have been seen by many historians as a period of rapid and irrevocable economic decline when the old Victorian economy 'crashed in ruins', resulting in mass unemployment. But others have depicted the two decades between the wars as a time of successful economic modernisation and of high productivity when living standards rose and affluence dawned.

The first essential is to realise the complexity of the seemingly simple question 'How did the economy perform between 1918 and 1939?'. Most historians would respond to this question with a whole series of their own. First, which sector(s) of the economy are we concerned with? The British economy was not monolithic (a single unit). Clearly we must look at as many different sectors of the economy as possible. At the very least we must consider the old staple industries and the new industries, like cars, electrical goods, and so on. But we should also look at the so-called 'service' industries, like transport, retailing, administration and entertainment, and the financial services sector, including Britain's overseas investments and 'invisible exports'. Nor should we forget agriculture, for if man cannot live by bread alone, it is certain that human beings cannot exist without food. All too often we can slip into the error of equating 'economy' with industry, to the neglect of agriculture. We should also be aware of the regional variations of the British economy. Parts of the country fared very differently from each other because different sectors of the economy were sited in them.

The next sub-question to be posed is how we measure economic 'performance'. Should we take account, above all else, of output – of the amounts being produced by industry and agriculture? If so, then gross domestic product (GDP) will be our main yardstick. But perhaps productivity (output per worker) is a better measure since it tends to reflect technological innovation and the 'modernisation' of industry. Should we emphasise the level of profits earned by industrialists? Or perhaps we should measure economic performance by the benefits that accrued more widely, in other words by the standard of living of the workers and their families? Perhaps levels of employment – and of unemployment – should also be taken into consideration. Might they even be considered the prime measure of economic well-being? The (uncomfortable) fact is that there are no universally accepted standards by which to measure economic performance. We must all of us therefore establish our own criteria. It is also important to see the British economy between 1918 and 1939 in perspective. This involves comparing its performance with earlier and later periods in British history (thus enabling us to see 'absolute' decline or progress) and with foreign economies (thus enabling us to see 'relative' decline or progress). An alternative is to try to compare actual economic performance with the optimum that could have been achieved. This is an interesting approach but also an extremely difficult one.

The final sub-question concerns the particular time within the period we are concerned with, for economic activity went in cycles. Economic historians often talk of the 'trade cycle' or 'business cycle'. These terms perhaps imply a greater regularity in the pattern of economic activity than is ever really the case, but they are useful nevertheless. Economic activity has 'troughs' and 'peaks' and thus can best be represented diagrammatically by curves rather than straight lines. Thus there was no 'typical' year between the wars, and there was no single pattern of decline or progress. Much therefore depends on precisely which part of the period we are considering.

Clearly there are difficulties in examining British economic performance between the wars, especially when we add the perennial question of the reliability of statistics to the above problems. Statistical data are probably more reliable for the inter-war years than for any previous period in British history, but even so we must always make allowances for the inadequacies and margins of error which statistics always contain and for the variety of ways in which they may be interpreted. Nevertheless, while being cautious, we should not be defeatist. We do in fact know a tremendous amount about the inter-war economy. For instance, most historians are agreed on the broad pattern of the trade cycle, with a peak just after the war giving way to a trough in 1921–2 and then a recovery until the worst depression of the period in 1929–32. Recovery then followed in 1933–7, before another minor downturn at the end of 1937. In 1938–9 rearmament produced further economic growth. It is most convenient to examine the economy within this broad chronological framework.

1 1918–22: the Post-war Years

a) Boom

There was great optimism at the end of 1918. People wanted to see a better and more fulfilling life for those who had survived the war. Lloyd George, the Prime Minister, won a general election on the slogans 'a land fit for heroes' and 'homes for heroes'. Such promises were immensely popular. The hard question was whether the economy could possibly allow their realisation and support a higher standard of living.

The war had contradictory effects on the British economy (see page 42). Many lives had been lost, much destruction had occurred and, moreover, vast debts had been accumulated. On the other hand, the war had given a new lease of life to the staple industries and had stimulated a large amount of modernisation. Were the overall results positive or negative? For a time it seemed that they were positive, and a boom occurred in Britain in 1919 and 1920. Civilian industries were restocking and pent-up consumer demand was great: British industry therefore expanded to satisfy this high level of demand. Similarly, export industries did well and it seemed that Britain would play a leading role in Europe's recovery from the devastation of war. All seemed set fair. Investment was high in staple industries like shipbuilding and textiles and there was little unemployment, so that in 1920 only 2.6 per cent of insured workers were without a job. Profits and wages were rising, and industrial production grew by about 20 per cent within two years of the end of the fighting. There was also a rise on the stock market.

b) Bust

It was all too good to last, and in the winter of 1920–21 the bubble burst. Production soon exceeded consumption and a brief but deep depression began. In December 1920 unemployment more than doubled, and in June 1921 it stood at over two million (18 per cent of the insured workforce). Industrial production slumped alarmingly: figures for 1921 were slightly lower than those for 1918, while exports declined by half during the year. Prices fell as sharply as they had risen, so that inflation was replaced by deflation – in other words, the prices of goods fell rather than rose, so that money was worth more not less. In fact the inter-war period were henceforth characterised by deflation.

The trouble stemmed in part from a world economic slump, but it was also due to peculiar British circumstances. During the war the urgent demand for the products of Britain's staple industries led to massive investment in these sectors of the economy, and this continued even after the war. But by 1921 it was clear that there had been substantial over-investment and that the boom had been fuelled by what the *Economist* called a 'craze for speculation'. Many companies had expanded rapidly but unwisely, borrowing large sums against the expectation of future profits that failed to materialise. Their confidence now looked short-sighted because the world no longer needed British staple goods in anything like the same quantities.

Britain's capacity to produce steel had expanded by 50 per cent during the war, but in the post-war period neither the domestic economy nor export orders could absorb such quantities. Too many other countries were producing their own steel. It was the same with shipping. During the war there had been an insatiable demand for ships, and it was hoped that in the post-war world the British shipbuilding industry would continue to be profitable. In 1920 Britain was building two million tons of shipping. But merchant vessels were no longer being sunk by enemy submarines, and soon shipbuilding had to be scaled back to little more than half a million tons a year. Nor was British coal such a valuable commodity after the war as before: not only were there other countries supplying coal to the world market, but gas and electricity had emerged as rival industrial fuels and ships had begun to be powered by oil. In addition, hydro-electric power had started to be exploited in Scotland and Wales. The textile industry suffered as well: overseas markets had been lost during the war to the Japanese and other competitors, and they could not be won back.

Even before the war the old staple industries had been relatively depressed, and it had been clear to observers that the British economy needed to diversify in order to regain its competitive edge. Now the war had produced significant over-capacity in these industries. As a result, in areas of the country like South Wales, the North-West and North-East of England and the Clydeside area of Scotland, there were soon massive lay-offs of workers. What economists term 'structural unemployment' had come to Britain: this was unemployment resulting from the structure of the British economy and not merely from a trough in the trade cycle. Mass unemployment in 1921–2 coincided with the downturn of the cycle, but when the recession ended a million men – including many miners, steel workers, shipbuilders and textile workers – were still without a job. While 'cyclical' unemployment by its very nature tends to be short-term, 'structural' unemployment is likely to be much longer-term. Many workers made redundant in 1921 were to remain unemployed throughout the inter-war period. There were at least a million people unemployed in Britain – the 'intractable ten per cent' of the insured workforce – from 1921 until 1940.

2 The Recovery of 1923–9

a) The Pessimistic View

According to several historians, the existence of this mass unemployment was the most significant fact about the whole inter-war economy. Given that over a million workers were continuously unemployed, it followed that the British economy was not performing at near full (or optimum) capacity. The employment record of 1923–9 looks especially poor when compared with other countries. In the United States the post-war boom lasted until 1929: these were the so-called 'Roaring Twenties'. The USA, of course, had not suffered from the war as Britain had, and so comparisons between the British and American economies may be unfair. But in France, too, 1923–9 was a time of economic expansion and high employment, and the French economy had suffered even more from the war than Britain's had. By 1928 there was full employment in France: fewer than 600 people were claiming unemployment benefit and several million immigrant workers had found jobs in French industry.

There is other evidence that the British economy performed badly in this period. In 1920–9 the value of Britain's imports exceeded that of her exports: there was a sizable 'current account' deficit. Britain's trading position was significantly weaker than before the war. In fact there was an overall balance of payments surplus because of Britain's 'invisible exports', but these were no longer nearly as lucrative as before 1914. The war, and then war debts and reparations, had helped to destroy the old international financial order which Britain had once dominated. The City of London could not win back its former position as financial capital of the world and, because some foreign investments had been sold during the war, profits from overseas investment income were lower than before 1914. The United States was now lending more money abroad than Britain, and the dollar replaced the pound as the dominant international currency. As a result, Britain had a smaller overall balance of payments surplus than before the war. A smaller proportion of GDP was also invested domestically than before the war, a worrying fact given that the new industries tended to be capital-intensive (relying on expensive machinery rather than on a large labour force). Put simply, it seems that Britain's relative decline continued after the war. During the 1920s Britain's share of world exports fell from just under 18 per cent to just under 11 per cent. Statistical indices show that while in 1929 British manufacturing production equalled that of 1913, US production had risen by 80 per cent, France's by 40 per cent and Japan's by 200 per cent. British economic decline in these years was, it has been said, 'a palpable fact'.

b) The Optimistic View

Yet there is a school of historians which emphasises the positive aspects of the mid-1920s. There was, according to one historian, 'a sort of boom' in this period. The City of London, for instance, may not have been as dominant in world finance as hitherto, but even so it continued to earn high profits and to put the balance of payments in the black. These historians, while admitting the high levels of unemployment, point out that despite under-utilised manpower the economy enjoyed considerable success. They estimate, for instance, that between 1920 and 1929 industrial production grew by an average of about 2.8 per cent a year, double the rate of growth of the pre-war years (1899–1913).

Indices of productivity are among the hardest to calculate. This is because it is so difficult to make allowances for the changing number of hours that people worked and also for the quality of the goods produced. Increases in productivity can also be misleading, since so much depends on the starting point of efficiency or inefficiency: an inefficient economy can make startling increases in productivity and still be less efficient than a rival economy, making much lower productivity increases but operating from a higher initial level. Nevertheless, according to the available data, the British economy achieved an excellent rate of productivity in the 1920s. Output per worker per hour expanded by an average of 3.8 per cent a year in this decade. Based on these figures, the British economy did better than most of its economic rivals.

No longer were the staple industries employing so many people, and no longer were they producing or exporting so much. But they enjoyed significant increases in productivity. In the mining industry productivity increased by a total of 18 per cent between 1924 and 1930, while in the iron and steel industry there were productivity increases of 25 per cent. In addition, major strides were made in the new industries, as investment shifted to electrical engineering, motor vehicles, chemicals, to new man-made fibres such as rayon (artificial silk), and to paper and printing. Imperial Chemical Industries (ICI) was founded in 1926. Such industries often adopted the most modern equipment and the most up-to-date production techniques, utilising the conveyor-belt system. This sector also experienced a large number of mergers of companies, which made for greater efficiency. For example, the number of car manufacturers fell by half in the 1920s, and over the same period output grew by a very healthy six per cent a year while the price of an average car fell by about one-third. Clearly, the overall figures which show that in 1929 Britain was producing only as much as in 1913 disguise the transformation of the economy that was beginning to take place.

One of the most important new factors producing growth in the 1920s was the Central Electricity Board, created in 1926. The Board gave an important impetus to the generation of electricity, so that a completely new network of power stations was built, and it also constructed a system of high-voltage transmission lines ('the national grid'). Not only did homes benefit – so that whereas in 1920 only one in 17 houses was wired for electricity, ten years later the figure had risen to one in three – but industry generally was profoundly affected. New electrically-powered industries were now set up away from coalfields, the traditional source of energy, and near to the largest consumer markets. A large-scale relocation of industry began, and the dominant sectors of the economy were soon sited in the Midlands and the South East. Furthermore, electricity produced a growth in consumer goods industries, as electrical appliances such as radios and vacuum cleaners became popular.

The 1920s have been called 'a watershed between the old industrial regime of the pre-1914 era and the new industrial economy of the post-1945 period'. This 'new' economy included a growing 'service' sector. Large retailing stores multiplied in the 1920s, so that Marks and Spencers, Boots, Woolworths and Sainsbury's all began, and the advertising industry became important. In the 1930s many of these developments continued apace, but in other respects a sharp break occurred in 1929.

3 The Great Depression, 1929–32

a) Origins

In 1929 the most severe depression of modern times began. Probably its longer-term origins were connected with the disruptive effects of the First World War. More specifically it stemmed from speculation on the Wall Street stock market in the United States. A mania for speculation pushed stocks and shares to record heights, so that fortunes were made very rapidly. Many people bought shares on credit, hoping to pay for them and make a profit by quick re-sales. The problem was that the inflated prices of shares bore little relation to the fundamental value of the companies they were supposed to represent. When confidence dipped in October 1929 the stock market crashed: 24 October was 'Black Thursday'. A loss of confidence made people sell their shares and so prices fell, which produced further falls in confidence and still more sales and still lower prices. A 'vicious circle' was created. By the end of the month American investors had lost $40,000 million. The stock market only stabilised when 80 per cent of its value had been lost. But the problems did not end there. Over the next years, thousands of American banks went bankrupt, the demand for goods fell, and unemployment rose to about 13 million in 1933.

The depression quickly reached the rest of the world. American bankers were no longer prepared to lend money abroad, while short-term US loans ('hot money') were recalled. Furthermore, American consumption fell, and as a result exports to the USA suffered badly. The lower demand for goods meant that their prices slumped. 'Primary products' (raw materials, as distinct from manufactured goods) were especially badly hit: producers tended to compensate for lower prices by exporting greater volumes, but the resulting glut on the world market only depressed prices still more. Almost everywhere unemployment increased as business confidence disappeared.

b) Effects on Britain

In Britain the value of exports virtually halved between 1929 and 1931, and there was a deficit on visible trade for which not even 'invisibles' could compensate. Over the same period unemployment mounted. The one million unemployed at the start of 1929 quickly doubled, and in 1931–2 almost three million people were out of work – about 22 per cent of the insured workforce. In addition, there were probably another 750,000 people unemployed who, for various reasons, did not register. In total, around six or seven million people, including dependants, lived on the dole in the worst months of the depression. Rates of unemployment were as bad in Britain as in the United States or Germany. The British economy was in crisis. No banks collapsed, as they did in America and continental Europe, but in 1931 there was an overall balance of payments deficit of £100 million which provoked a political crisis that saw the downfall of the second Labour government (see pages 109–112).

Many at the time thought that this depression was not just a particularly acute trough in the trade cycle. It seemed worse than that, and only the most optimistic commentators could foresee an end to it all. The pessimists believed that the whole capitalist system was breaking down.

4 Economic Recovery, 1932–9

Britain's economic performance between 1932 and 1939 has been the subject of extensive debate. As for the 1920s, there has been a divergence of opinion between the 'pessimists', who have stressed the gloomier aspects of the period (including high unemployment and the further decline of the old staple industries), and the 'optimists', who have drawn attention to areas of improvement (including the growth of new consumer goods industries and high levels of productivity). The Thirties have been seen as a period of economic stagnation by some and of substantial economic progress by others. Not surprisingly, each of the two schools of thought has to a large extent concentrated on different aspects of these years, and many recent writers have tried to show that the two views are in fact complementary rather than contradictory. The 1930s are often seen now as 'a decade of contrasts', a period of paradox. The years 1932–9 were very varied economically.

a) Levels of Unemployment

Unemployment totals give a useful indication of the severity of the depression and of recovery from it. The peak of the depression was reached in the early months of 1932, when almost three million people were out of work. Thereafter the increase in employment, while never spectacular, was steady (provided seasonal variations, stemming from the fact that fewer people are generally employed in the building and other trades in the winter months, are ignored). Only in 1937–8 was the trend disturbed, as the trade cycle turned downwards, but this was a short-lived disturbance. Nevertheless in 1939 there were still a million and a half people out of work.

Average unemployment totals

1932 – 2,700,000	1936 – 1,600,000
1933 – 2,500,000	1937 – 1,500,000
1934 – 2,200,000	1938 – 1,900,000
1935 – 2,000,000	1939 – 1,500,000

These figures are useful: although they tell us about only one aspect of the economy in the 1930s, they show that there was undoubtedly some sort of recovery. But, as *national* totals, they tell us nothing about the *regional* pattern of employment.

b) The Depressed Areas

The staple industries, already suffering from structural unemployment in the 1920s, were badly hit by the depression of the early 1930s. Export orders fell, and consequently these industries suffered unemployment levels far higher than the national averages. In 1932, when a national average 22 per cent of workers were unemployed, 35 per cent of coalminers were out of work, as were 46 per cent of iron and steel workers and 62 per cent of shipbuilders and repairers. In individual towns, especially those economically dependent on a single ailing industry, totals were especially high. In 1934 62 per cent of workers were unemployed in Merthyr Tydfil in South Wales which was dependent on mining. In Jarrow, in the North East, where Palmers' shipbuilding yard had closed down, 73 per cent were out of a job in 1935.

For the rest of the 1930s the staple industries continued to suffer from economic depression. Indeed, in some ways the situation became worse than ever. In the cotton industry, for example, where production had already fallen by 25 per cent in 1910–20, and then by almost 50 per cent in the following decade, exports fell from 3,800 million square yards in 1929 to 2,000 million in 1937. India, which had been the great market for Lancashire textiles in the previous century, was now exporting cotton goods to Britain. It was a similar story with shipbuilding. Orders for British ships dropped badly in the 1930s, so that in 1936 Britain actually imported more ships than it exported.

The concentration of the staple industries in certain areas of the country meant that unemployment in the 1930s was a regional phenomenon, once the worst of the depression was over. There were exceptions (pockets of prosperity) within this broad pattern, but these (like Halifax in Yorkshire, centre of a flourishing machine tool trade) were the proverbial exceptions that prove the rule. The 'depressed areas' were born (see the map on page 56). These parts of the country suffered the worst housing, the lowest standards of health, and significantly higher rates of infant and maternal mortality, as well as a migration of people to other parts of the country.

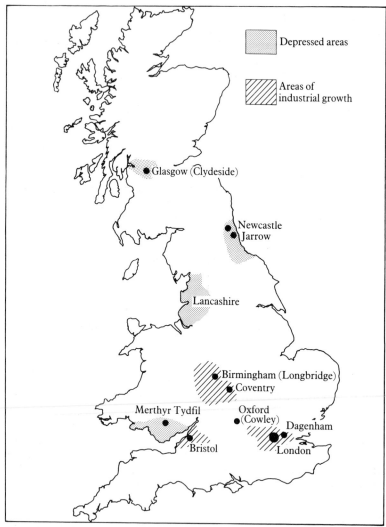

Industry in the 1930s

The 'optimists' point out that even in these areas of the country there were some signs of economic growth. Steel production, for example, rose from a trough of 5.2 million tons in 1932 to reach seven million tons in 1933 and 13 million tons in 1937. Britain's share of world output was rising and the industry was being made more efficient. There were also important advances in the coal industry. British pits could not regain their pre-war export markets, and nor did they produce as much in the 1930s as at the end of the 1920s, but productivity reached new heights. Output per man rose by over one-third between 1924 and 1938, and by the end of the decade over 60 per cent of coal was cut by machinery. However, such developments need to be seen in a European context. Productivity increased at least twice as rapidly over the same years in continental mines as in Britain. In the Ruhr, in Germany, 97 per cent of coal was cut by mechanical means as early as 1934.

c) Economic Revival: the New and Service Industries

There is disagreement about just how badly the Great Depression hit this country. The 'optimists' point out that whereas world output fell by almost 30 per cent between 1929 and 1932, Britain's declined by only half this figure, while the 'pessimists' reply that this was simply a consequence of the fact that the British economy had not undergone a boom in the late-1920s: having risen less steeply than its rivals, it had less far to fall. However, all are agreed that there was a significant revival of output in the 1930s, as the following table indicates.

Index of Production

1929 – 100 (an index figure)	1934 – 104
1930 – 92	1935 – 110
1931 – 84	1936 – 118
1932 – 85	1937 – 124
1933 – 93	

We can thus see that between 1932 and 1937 industrial production rose by 46 per cent. One feature of this was the continued development of the electricity industry. In 1930 one in three houses was supplied with electricity, but in 1939 two out of three houses were wired for supply. By this time 325,000 people worked for the electricity industry, and probably the same number were employed in electrical engineering, helping to produce the new range of electrically-powered consumer goods. The consumption of electricity doubled between 1931 and 1937. The number of electric cookers sold increased from 75,000 in 1930 to 250,000 in 1935, and the number of radios from 500,000 in 1930 to two million in 1937.

A report of 1938 highlighted the degree to which the electricity industry generated prosperity:

1 The greatest single factor in the post-slump situation has been the entrance into operation of the Grid under the control of the Central Electricity Board . . . The last tower of the Grid was erected in September, 1933. Since then there have been additions

5 to the transmission system and some expansion of transforming
and switching equipment of the substations. At the end of 1937,
however, the Grid comprised about 4,180 miles of primary and
secondary transmission lines, linking up selected generating
stations with a capacity of over $7\frac{1}{2}$ million kilowatts . . .
10 The total cost of erecting the transmission system, exclusive of
capitalised interest, was about £27,800,000, and the greater part
of the expenditure involved was allocated during the slump years,
1930 to 1933, so that the Board was able to take advantage of
falling prices, which made the cost of construction come very
15 close to the estimates calculated in 1927, to carry out a slightly
more ambitious scheme without additional cost, and to keep the
manufacturing workshops at a steady level of activity.

The motor-vehicle industry was another success story of the 1930s.
Three firms – Morris at Cowley in Oxford, Ford at Dagenham in Essex
and Austin at Longbridge in Birmingham – dominated production, and
output rose from 95,000 vehicles in 1923 to over half a million in 1937.
The number of vehicles on the roads doubled between 1930 and 1939,
from one and a half million to over three million. By the latter date
there were around 400,000 people employed in the industry. The
aircraft industry also expanded considerably, at Coventry and Bristol,
and so did chemical giants like Imperial Chemical Industries (ICI),
which even set up a factory at Jarrow in the late 1930s. More typically,
however, the new industries tended to be sited in the South East and
the Midlands (see the map on page 56), rather than in the depressed
areas of the country: 80 per cent of new factories built between 1932
and 1937 were in Greater London, by which time about one-fifth of
Britain's population lived within a 15-mile radius of Charing Cross
(with consequent problems of congestion). Not only did the new
factories provide jobs in this area, but so too did the new service
industries that grew up as a consequence – retailing, insurance,
advertising, and forms of entertainment such as the cinema. Such
service industries increased their work force even during the worst
years of the depression.

d) The Housing Boom

Another source of growth in the economy was the 'housing boom' of the
1930s. In the 1920s an average of 150,000 new houses had been
completed each year in England and Wales, but from 1930 onwards
there was a substantial increase in the numbers of houses and flats built.
Even during the worst years of depression (1931 and 1932), 200,000
houses were constructed each year in England and Wales, and for the
rest of the decade significantly more dwellings were erected. In the
Thirties as a whole, 2.7 million were built. There were several reasons

for this: building costs (and especially the price of imported timber) fell during the depression and also the construction industry became more efficient. In addition investment in building societies rose eightfold in the inter-war period, so that it became relatively easy to obtain cheap mortgages (at around four and a half per cent interest) and now they could be extended over a longer period (typically 25 years rather than 16). The 1930s have been called 'probably the most favourable period for house purchase in the twentieth century'. Priced at around £450 for a semi-detached house, twice the annual salary of a professional man, new houses were now within the range of most middle-class and some working-class families.

   Not surprisingly, the number of workers employed in the building industry increased by almost one-third in the 1930s, while the housing boom also led to further employment in trades supplying building materials. New houses were wired for electricity, and so the electricity industry was also stimulated. Often the new houses were sited in the suburbs of major cities, and as a result the transportation system (the 'economic infrastructure') – including new electric railways in the South – was modernised.

e) 1937–8: a Temporary Brake

In the autumn of 1937 the business cycle dipped, and it seemed that the economy might be about to go into recession. In the worst months of 1938 unemployment reached almost two million, and in the year as a whole industrial production fell and the balance of payments deficit worsened. But the downswing proved short-lived, mainly because by this time the government had embarked on a rearmament programme that stimulated British industry. Between 1935 and 1939 rearmament created around one million new jobs. Hence the inter-war period ended with a relatively buoyant economy. Even the number of unemployed had declined. In 1939 an average of 7.9 per cent of the insured workforce were unemployed, the lowest figure since 1920. Yet even so, the number of unemployed was not to fall below one million until the spring of 1940. The main economic problem of the whole inter-war period had not been solved.

5 Causes of Economic Recovery

a) The Trade Cycle

Most historians agree that there was a recovery after the Great Depression, but there is no consensus about the causes of this upturn. Some say that the 'natural' recovery of the trade cycle was responsible. This view is supported by the fact that the autumn of 1937 saw the ending of the upward curve of the cycle – a sure sign that recovery was at least partly cyclical – and also by the fact that the recovery was on a world-wide scale. According to this view, there is no great mystery about such recovery as occurred: it owed much more to external factors than to any internal strength of the British economy. It has even been said, by the pessimists, that without the artificial stimulus provided by rearmament, unemployment might have risen to three million by 1939. However, most historians would argue that there were other causes of the recovery besides the operation of the trade cycle.

b) The New Industries

Several historians have pointed to the dynamic role of the new industries, which they see as a significant force producing recovery. But there are problems with this view. First there is the question of definition. What exactly was a 'new' industry? Some industries which have been classified as new (such as rayon production) were very much out-growths of 'old' industries (textiles, in the case of rayon). There has also been a tendency to define 'new' as 'expanding' – in which case it is scarcely surprising that the 'new' industries seem to have spearheaded industrial growth! Above all, the criticism has been made that the new industries constituted too small a portion of British industry to account for the recovery: they were responsible for only seven per cent of employment in 1934 and for only about 20 per cent of output in 1935. They were also sometimes far less efficient than is generally supposed: the chemical giant ICI, for instance, invested £20 million in a fertiliser plant – an amount equivalent to one-third of all capital investment in manufacturing industry in that year – but soon had to write off the whole amount as a total failure. Furthermore, the newer industries may have grown most strongly after the vital 1932–4 period in which the depression ended. They may thus have sustained rather than started the recovery.

Nevertheless, it is clear that the new industries were a growing and significant force within the economy, even though the staple industries constituted a larger part of the total economy. (The staple industries accounted for 37 per cent of British industrial production in 1924 and 28 per cent in 1935, while over the same period the percentage of industrial production for which the new industries were responsible increased from 14 to 20 per cent.) Did the new industries lift the economy out of recession? Most historians would judge that while they probably did not, they nevertheless contributed to recovery. The roles of the electricity and car industries were especially significant.

c) The Housing Boom

The 'housing boom' has also been seen as a major factor in British recovery. It undoubtedly had a significant effect, and by 1935 (the peak year for construction) a high proportion of all investment in Britain went into housing. Building and allied trades absorbed an extra three-quarters of a million workers between 1932 and 1934. But perhaps this factor was in turn made possible by others, including population movements, mortgage availability and low interest rates (see page 116). Some believe that a regular building cycle of about 20 years' duration existed. House-building involved so many allied industries (cement, electricity, plumbing, and so on) that it has been said that building alone cannot have been responsible for recovery: the allied trades must have already been in relatively good shape. Nevertheless few would deny that the housing boom was another important factor in Britain's economic growth in the 1930s.

d) Affluence and Consumer Spending

Clearly Britain's economic recovery from the Great Depression depended in large measure on the ability and willingness of people to spend – to purchase new houses and to buy the increasing range of consumer goods that were on offer. It has been said that the 1930s saw a 'consumer-led' recovery. This in turn depended on the existence of a greater degree of 'disposable income' (that is, a surplus after expenditure on basic necessities) among British people. The Ministry of Labour established that in 1938 an average family had double the real income of a family in 1913–14. This should be an important factor in any assessment of the British economy after the war. Those in work in the 1930s were progressively better off as the decade proceeded since, although wage rates fell, continuing deflation meant that the cost of living fell more steeply. The result was a significant rise in living standards. During the Thirties, average real wages probably rose by about 15 per cent.

A major factor in this higher standard of living was a fall in the cost of goods that resulted from more efficient methods of production and also from a steep fall in the price of imported raw materials. The 'terms of trade' (a comparison between the relative costs of Britain's exports and imports) moved in Britain's favour in the 1930s: for a given volume of exports Britain could purchase an expanding volume of imports. For example, in 1936 Britain was importing almost exactly the same volume of goods as in 1929 but their cost was 32 per cent less. Put another way, Britain's new higher standard of living was purchased at the price of lower standards in 'third world' countries. Another factor was the smaller size of British families. The average number of children per family declined from 4.2 in 1929 to 3.2 in 1939. Smaller family size meant greater disposable income. This is seen most vividly not only in the greater number of consumer goods that could be afforded but in the amounts spent on entertainment and holidays. The 1930s were the heyday of the cinema: by the end of the decade over 20 million tickets were sold each week at Britain's 5,000 cinemas. Scarcely less important to many people was the annual holiday. During the 1930s the number of people entitled to a paid holiday increased from about one and a half million to over 11 million, and by the end of the decade around 20 million people visited the seaside every year. Billy Butlin opened his first holiday camps in the years before the Second World War. The number of jobs in entertainment and sport grew, between 1930 and 1937, from 65,000 to 116,000, while those in hotels and restaurants increased from 300,000 to 380,000.

6 The 1930s: a Conclusion

Mass unemployment was a personal tragedy for millions of people in the 1930s. Lives were blighted and human potential was wasted. Many of the unemployed felt that, to the politicians at Westminster, they were merely statistics. Unfortunately it is easy for historians to consider them in the same way, as so many units in an economic equation. There is a perennial danger that historians – and especially economic historians, to whom individual life-stories can seldom be as significant as large-scale (macro-)economic trends – will fail to see the human reality that underlies their studies. It often requires a conscious effort to realise the human significance of statistical and other data.

Unemployment should also be at the centre of our study of British economic performance for another reason: it reveals that the economy was operating at considerably below its optimum level. As we have seen, there are various ways of assessing British economic performance – in comparison with that of its competitors, for instance, or with other periods in British history. Another way is to construct a 'counterfactual model' (as opposed to the 'factual' record of what was achieved). This is a highly complicated undertaking. It involves assessing how Britain could have performed economically at an optimum level, given its raw materials, its population, the availability of markets, consumption habits and so on. The clearest fact of all to emerge from the construction of such a model is that an economy cannot operate at anything like full efficiency when over ten per cent of its workers are unemployed. Well over a million workers were unproductive in the 1930s and had to be supported by unemployment benefit. In addition, they were unable to stimulate economic growth because they could not afford to buy many goods or services. The unemployed were thus an economic liability, whereas in work they would have been an asset. It can also be argued that the existence of such a large number of unemployed people tended to keep down wage rates for those in work, since workers who refused to accept existing wage levels could be replaced by the 'reserve army of the unemployed'. As a result, living standards in general were lower than they otherwise might have been.

However, we should not allow a justified concentration on unemployment to produce an unjustified and unbalanced picture of the economy as a whole. There were other failures, besides unemployment. The staple industries declined significantly, and in addition the balance of payments situation was unfavourable. From 1930 to 1938 there was an annual average deficit on visible trade of £255 million, which was only partially offset by annual surpluses from invisible earnings averaging £216 million. On the other hand, there were considerable economic successes in the 1930s, especially in the growth of new consumer goods industries. Those who praise the economic performance of the 1930s would say that the economy was undergoing a painful but necessary period of economic readjustment: in other words, the economy had to switch from producing what people did not want to supplying what they did. Thus unemployment, while a personal tragedy to those thrown out of work, can be seen as an inevitable consequence of a necessary economic reorientation. According to this view, the 'decline' of the staple industries should be seen not as a failure of the 1930s but, paradoxically, almost as a success! The staple industries had to decline, to employ fewer people and to match their output to consumers' needs. The key issue was whether as they became leaner they also became fitter and more competitive. The iron and steel industry undoubtedly did.

The annual growth rate for British industry in the 1930s was between 2.3 and 3.3 per cent (a substantial achievement) and between 1932 and 1937 industrial output rose by almost 50 per cent. Britain may have fallen behind its rivals in industrial growth in the 1920s, but this was not the case in the 1930s. Its rate of growth outstripped that of the United States and France. By 1939 Britain was fourth in the world table of industrial producers, behind the USA, the USSR and Germany, all larger and 'naturally' stronger competitors. Behind Britain – a long way behind – came rivals of more equal size and resources. In 1939 Britain was producing twice as much as France, two and a half times as much as Japan, and over three times as much as Italy. Britain's share of world trade in the 1930s varied from year to year (9.36 per cent was the lowest in 1931, 11.08 per cent the highest in 1935), but it had very probably ceased to decline.

7 The Inter-war Period as a Whole

a) Agriculture

Agriculture was a small sector of the economy, producing no more than four per cent of Britain's national income and employing between five and seven per cent of the British workforce, but it should not be entirely overlooked. Before 1914 British agriculture had been in decline: prices were low and around 55 per cent (by value) of all foods consumed in Britain were imported. During the war, when imports were cut back, production of food had expanded rapidly and it was hoped that in the post-war period food production could be permanently increased so that the import bill might be reduced. In fact these hopes were not fulfilled. World food prices fell in 1921 and again in 1929, acting as a disincentive to farmers. Food production in Britain increased by about four per cent between 1925 and 1930, largely owing to higher yields per acre, but by the latter date the percentage of food that was imported had risen to 60.

In the 1930s there was again increased output. Between 1931 and 1937 production rose by about one-sixth. This was largely because attempts were made to utilise more scientific methods (thus improving yields) and to introduce greater mechanisation. The number of tractors in England and Wales increased from 16,500 in 1925 to 40,000 in 1937, while over the same period the number of working horses declined; but even so there were still about 20 times more horses than tractors in the mid-1930s. Indeed, Britain had one of the least mechanised farming systems of the economically advanced nations. It was not until the Second World War that there was a real modernisation of British agriculture. Between 1939 and 1945 the number of tractors and combine harvesters on British farms increased by 400 per cent.

In the 1930s under the stimulus of government subsidies reaching more than £100 million a year, there were modest increases in farming efficiency. The number of farm workers fell by about a third (from seven per cent to five per cent of the total workforce), the acreage under cultivation fell marginally (by about five per cent), and yet production increased. At the end of the period Britain imported about 50 per cent of its food, less than before the First World War. There had therefore been increases in productivity. Yet, although British agriculture between the wars was certainly not a story of failure, few have ventured to call it a success.

b) Industry

Britain's industrial performance between 1918 and 1939 was very varied, and it is thus very difficult to generalise about it. Indeed, even to talk about what happened in 'staple' and 'new' industries is to ignore the very real differences that existed between different trades within these two broad sectors – and within the single trades there were firms that performed very differently. There were also considerable regional variations, while the fluctuations of the trade cycle meant that there was considerable change over time, rather than a linear pattern towards greater poverty or affluence. The diversity was such that evidence can be provided for any number of generalisations about British industrial performance. We must therefore be cautious and qualified in our assessment.

The inter-war period was a paradoxical one economically. Many people began to experience affluence for the first time, while others

were condemned to life on the dole. In 1933 the novelist J.B. Priestley
toured England:

1 I had seen England. I had seen a lot of Englands. How many? At
once three disengaged themselves from the shifting mass. There
was, first, Old England, the country of the cathedrals and manor
houses and inns, of Parson and Squire . . . We all know this
5 England, which at its best cannot be improved upon in this
world. That is, as a country to lounge about in . . . It has long
ceased to earn its own living . . .
    Then, I decided, there is the nineteenth-century England, the
industrial England of coal, iron, steel, cotton, wool, railways; of
10 thousands of rows of little houses all alike . . . This England . . . is
not being added to and has no new life poured into it . . . It
provided a good parade ground for tough, enterprising men, who
would build their factories in the knowledge that the world was
waiting for their products, and who also knew that once they had
15 accumulated a tidy fortune they could slip out of this mucky
England of their making . . .
    The third England, I concluded, was the new post-war Eng-
land, belonging far more to the age itself than to the particular
island. America, I supposed, was its real birth-place. This is the
20 England of arterial and by-pass roads, of filling stations and
factories that look like exhibition buildings, of giant cinemas and
dance halls and cafés, bungalows and tiny garages, cocktail bars,
Woolworths, motor-coaches, wireless, hiking, factory girls look-
ing like actresses, greyhound racing and dirt tracks, swimming
25 pools and everything given away for cigarette coupons . . . It is a
large-scale, mass-production job, with cut prices. You could
almost accept Woolworths as its symbol.

It is undoubtedly preferable to stress the variety of Britain between
the wars rather than to convey a one-sided picture of affluence or
depression. There were riches and poverty, boom and bust. It was both
'the best of times' and 'the worst of times'. These phrases can of course
be applied to virtually every period in human history: at all times there
are positive and negative features to human society. Every buoyant
economy contains elements of stagnation, and every declining economy
nevertheless exhibits some progressive traits. The key question is
always the relative importance of the positive and negative features. In
the inter-war years both were vital. There were probably twice as many
coalminers as car-workers in the mid-1930s, and thus we cannot ignore
the relatively stagnant sectors of the economy. The new industries, on
the other hand, while more capital-intensive, contributed significantly
to Britain's production. For millions of people the inter-war years were
a time of poverty and distress, and yet for millions of other people there

was unparalleled affluence and opportunity. We must therefore give virtually equal weight to poverty and riches and reach a conclusion which is not indefinite or vague but decidedly two-sided.

The other issue to be addressed is the overall degree of change in the economy by the end of the inter-war period. It is true that the trade cycle ruled out any straight-line economic progress; but on the other hand one cycle was followed by another, and by the end of the inter-war period it was clear that the economy had undergone significant development. No longer was Britain pre-eminently an exporting economy. Most of the growth generated in the inter-war period had been due to domestic consumption. This was an important change. Exports from the 'staple industries' (a term that had become an anachronism) had fallen alarmingly, and indeed not since 1851 had Lancashire exported so little. Exports never recovered to their 1913 level between the wars, and the 1929 level was not equalled for the rest of the period, despite the fact that by 1937 British economic production was 20 per cent higher than in 1929 (see the table on page 57). The Victorian economy had indeed 'crashed in ruins' between the wars. But another economy had taken its place, based on new mass production and capable of producing higher rates of growth than in 1900–13. Despite large-scale unemployment, total output per head of the population probably grew between 1924 and 1937 by a third, faster in fact than in the heyday of Victorian England. This was a substantial achievement, especially since more people were now engaged in the non-productive 'service' industries, an achievement obscured for too long by the tenacious, one-sided popular image of the 1930s as 'the devil's decade' of unemployment and political failure.

For a time in the 1930s Britain's relative economic decline seemed to have been halted. Britain had come to rest, after a decline (*vis-à-vis* its rivals) that had been under way since the 1880s. Or so it seemed. In retrospect, we know it was merely a pause before another catastrophic world war and further decline. But the pause was a measure of the economic success of the inter-war years. Perhaps much more might have been achieved. It is often said that even the most progressive British firms tended to neglect management training and failed to invest sufficiently in industrial research. In addition, we can only wonder at how much greater the success might have been had governments tackled Britain's economic problems more effectively and had industrial relations been more harmonious.

Making notes on 'The Inter-war Years: an Economy in Decline?'

You need a detailed set of notes on this chapter. The headings and sub-headings should help you to organise your notes efficiently. Within

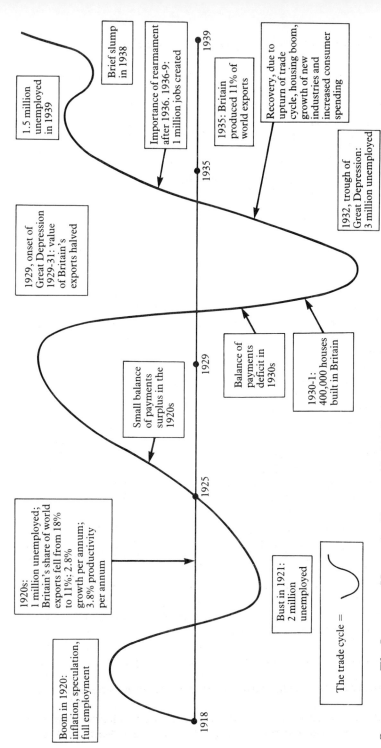

Boom in 1920: inflation, speculation, full employment

1920s: 1 million unemployed; Britain's share of world exports fell from 18% to 11%; 2.8% growth per annum; 3.8% productivity per annum

Bust in 1921: 2 million unemployed

The trade cycle =

Small balance of payments surplus in the 1920s

Balance of payments deficit in 1930s

1930-1: 400,000 houses built in Britain

1929, onset of Great Depression 1929-31: value of Britain's exports halved

1932, trough of Great Depression: 3 million unemployed

1935: Britain produced 11% of world exports

Recovery, due to upturn of trade cycle, housing boom, growth of new industries and increased consumer spending

1.5 million unemployed in 1939

Brief slump in 1938

Importance of rearmament after 1936. 1936-9: 1 million jobs created

1918   1925   1929   1935   1939

Summary – The Inter-war Years: An Economy in Decline?

each chronological division, you should note (i) the main economic developments, (ii) the ways in which economic changes can be assessed and interpreted, and (iii) the broad explanations of why economic change occurred.

As in previous chapters, the concluding sections are worth particular attention. Here you should think through the issues as thoroughly as possible and formulate your own views. Also as in previous chapters, add to your set of definitions of key phrases.

Finally, a word of warning. It is very easy when making notes on economic developments to lose the significance of figures by being too brief. If you are dealing with output, for instance, always remember to note not merely production totals but the period over which they are measured. Such accuracy is essential: it makes the difference between conveying sense and nonsense. You might write down that in a certain industry production increased by ten per cent – but does this mean per annum or over a set period of years? Also, remember to specify which units things are measured in: there is a big difference between pounds, kilograms, tons, and so on.

Answering essay questions on 'The Inter-war Years: an Economy in Decline?'

This is a popular topic for exam questions. A wide variety of questions is asked on the inter-war period as a whole. For instance:

1 To what extent should the period 1918–39 be seen as one of British economic decline?
2 Were the inter-war years characterised by depression or reconstruction for the British economy?
3 Account for the persistently high levels of unemployment that existed in Britain from 1921 to 1939.

Construct an essay plan for each of these titles. In particular work out ways of dividing up the material into manageable sections, on each of which you could write a paragraph. It is also worth spending time thinking about the main interpretation you would put forward to answer questions 1 and 2. Both of these questions ask about the relative importance of the 'positive' and 'negative' aspects of the inter-war economy. Would you give them equal weight or assign more prominence to one or the other? Remember the importance of establishing the criteria on which judgements are based. The third title is different from the others, demanding a knowledge of the economic factors that produced both structural and cyclical unemployment, but also of government policies that affected employment levels (an issue dealt with in Chapter 6).

Questions can also centre on the 1920s, but far more common are questions on the 1930s:

4 'By 1939 Britain had only partially recovered from the depression of the early 1930s.' Discuss.
5 Do you agree that Britain's recovery from the depression of the 1930s was regional rather than national?
6 To what extent was the decade of the 1930s one of economic gloom in Britain?

Variants of these questions are extremely common. It is worth thinking how you might tackle the final paragraph of each of them. Try to provide a succinct six to eight line conclusion to each. Remember that your answer must reflect the different types of questions asked. With the first type, which merely asks you to discuss a quotation, you are given a wide degree of latitude: but, even so, you must centre your discussion on the statement quoted. Do you agree with the view? If so, say so directly, and then comment on the degree of partial recovery as well as its sources. Perhaps you might think that 'partial' recovery for Britain as a whole stemmed from 'complete' recovery in certain areas, or maybe you think the word 'recovery' is misleading in its implication of a 'return to a former condition'. For the second question, you obviously have to answer a direct question: you can say yes or no; or, more likely, you will say 'yes' (to some extent and in certain respects) and 'no' (in others). For the third question, you must find a form of words to define the extent to which negative economic factors dominated the 1930s, taking account of regional variations and change over time. It is not easy to formulate adequate conclusions – all that is stressed here is the absolute necessity of tackling the key issues, instead of spoiling an essay by failing to address them.

Source-based questions on 'The Inter-War Years: an Economy in Decline?'

1 1938 report on electricity
Read the report on the electricity industry on pages 57–8 and answer the following questions:
a) To what other information would you need to have access in order to assess the significance of the figures specifying the length of the National Grid and the capacity of generating stations (lines 7–9)? *(6 marks)*

b) Explain how 'falling prices' (line 14) affected the profitability of the electricity industry. *(2 marks)*

c) How justified do you think the author of the report was in claiming that the Central Electricity Board and the National Grid constituted the 'greatest single factor' (line 1) in industrial recovery? Explain your answer. *(7 marks)*

2 Priestley's journey

Read the extracts from J.B. Priestley on page 65 and answer the following questions:

a) Priestley wrote of three Englands. Explain where each would have been located geographically. *(4 marks)*

b) Why did Priestley suggest that Woolworths might be an appropriate symbol of the third England (line 26)? *(4 marks)*

c) Which of the three Englands do you think Priestley was most sympathetically disposed towards? Explain your answer, using quotations from the extract. *(6 marks)*

d) Priestley claimed to have discovered 'at least' three Englands. Suggest one other England, besides the three specified, that he might have had in mind. *(1 mark)*

CHAPTER 5

The General Strike and Industrial Relations Between the Wars

1 Post-war Crisis, 1918–21

The end of the war saw a return to traditional industrial procedures. The Restoration of Pre-war Practices Act of 1919 meant that women lost their places in industry to the men whose jobs they had taken, and at the same time 'dilution' ceased to be compulsory. Industrial courts, as set up during the war, still existed, but it was no longer obligatory to submit disputes for their judgement. Nor were joint industrial councils continued, except in the civil service. As a result, 1918–21 also saw a return to pre-war industrial bitterness and confrontation. There was greater industrial conflict than in any previous period of British history.

After the war the trade union movement was stronger than ever before, with eight million members in 1921 – about 48 per cent of the labour force, compared with only 20 per cent before the war. Allied with this strength went a mood of militancy, resulting in a new wave of strikes. In 1919 35 million working days were lost in disputes, and in the following year almost 27 million. The climax was reached in 1921 with a massive 85 million working days lost. This was over twice as many as in the worst pre-war year. Perhaps not surprisingly, the government began to fear that British workers might follow the example set in Russia, where the Communists under Lenin had seized power in a revolution in 1917. The Prime Minister was told at the end of 1918 that there would be 'some sort of revolution' within the next 12 months. Another ominous sign was the formation of the Communist Party of Great Britain in 1920.

a) 'Red Clydeside'

After the war, British workers showed far less deference than previously to their 'superiors'. Even the police went on strike in 1919, and it was feared that the army might refuse to obey orders, especially if called upon to act against British workers. The armed forces were put to the test on the Clyde, where the shop stewards' movement had been powerful during the war.

A strike for a 40-hour week began in Glasgow in January 1919, and the red flag was raised from the town hall. 70,000 workers stopped work, and a few days later – on what became known as 'Bloody Friday' – a riot began when police baton-charged a crowd in George Square. At a time when left-wing coups were being attempted in Germany and elsewhere, the government and Special Branch detectives took these events very seriously, and many spoke of a Bolshevik revolution. As a result, 12,000 troops armed with machine guns, together with 100 lorries and six tanks, were sent into Glasgow. They obeyed orders without question and the situation was soon calmed. But the leaders of the strike received only light prison sentences: neither the jury nor the judge at their trial believed that they had really been planning a revolution, and the head of Special Branch was accused of being unduly alarmist.

Despite the syndicalist rhetoric of many shop stewards, government fears of revolution were exaggerated. Most of the strikes of this period were due to the rising cost of living. They were also unofficial rather than official stoppages, and soon trade union leaders began to regain control of their members. In 1920 the Trades Union Congress (TUC) – the 'parliament' of the trade union movement – was reformed. Previously it had been more an annual event than a permanent institution, but now it formed a General Council of about 30 members 'to co-ordinate industrial action'. However, this was not a sinister development, as some feared it would be. The General Council was soon dominated by moderates like Walter Citrine, its first general secretary. Nor was the tendency of unions to amalgamate necessarily a dangerous sign. In 1922, for instance, 14 unions and around 300,000 workers amalgamated to form the Transport and General Workers' Union; but its founder, Ernest Bevin, was another moderate who hoped to win better pay and conditions by reasoned argument rather than by confrontation. Bevin had taken the dockers' case for a minimum wage to a court of inquiry in 1920 and had argued his case brilliantly, actually buying and placing before the court the amount of food a docker's wages could buy. To highlight the contrast in diet, he also produced a menu from the restaurant of the Savoy Hotel! Similarly, many of the strikes of the period owed as much to the intransigence of employers as to worker militancy. Yet government fears were understandable since many workers voiced political as well as industrial demands. In May 1920 dockers refused to load a ship, the *Jolly George*, which they believed was to take weapons to the Poles in their war with communist Russia. This 'Hands off Russia' campaign achieved widespread support within the the Labour movement. More significantly, miners were calling not just for higher wages or better conditions of work but for the nationalisation of the coal mines of Great Britain.

2 The Miners and 'Black Friday'

The government had taken control of the mines during the war in an attempt to prevent strikes and to maximise production, and most miners now wanted full-scale nationalisation. Only this, they believed, would lead to better and safer conditions of work and to the mechanisation of their technologically-backward industry. Already government control had brought about a national wages agreement – so that miners all over the country received the same wages for the same work – rather than the local agreements the owners had favoured. In February 1919 the Miners' Federation of Great Britain called for wage rises and for nationalisation and, after a ballot of the members, threatened a strike. It seemed that they might be supported by the other two members of the 'triple alliance', the railwaymen and transport workers. The government then took action. There was at this time a shortage of coal in Europe, so that prices were high and more miners than ever before were employed (one and a quarter million, about one-tenth of the entire British work force). A strike at this point would have been especially serious. The government therefore headed off a menacing confrontation by appointing a commission under the chairmanship of a judge, Sir John Sankey, to investigate and to make recommendations on the issues.

The evidence collected by the Sankey Commission created a sensation. It revealed the high profits made during the war, the scandalously low living conditions of many miners and their families (whose houses were 'a reproach to our civilisation'), and the chaotic and fragmented structure of the industry, with around 3,000 pits owned by 1,500 individuals or companies. There were also about 4,000 landowners to whom a royalty had to be paid for every ton of coal raised to the surface. The Commission made recommendations for wage rises and a shorter working day of seven rather than eight hours: both were accepted by the government. But on the crucial issue of nationalisation there was no consensus. The commissioners were deadlocked, and so Sankey had to use his casting vote. He cast it in favour of nationalisation, but the government refused to take action. The miners, in the words of one of their spokesmen, then felt 'deceived, betrayed, duped'.

The government of the day was a coalition dominated by Conservatives, and to them nationalisation was anathema. The Prime Minister, Lloyd George, who was a Liberal, therefore had little choice but to reject the Sankey proposals; and when the boom gave way to slump, so that the price of coal was halved and the industry began operating at a loss, he hastily handed the mines back to their owners. On the day of decontrol, 1 April 1921, a national miners' strike began. The owners tried to institute pay cuts, on local rather than national scales, but the men would have none of it. Lloyd George had skilfully delayed a strike until the post-war boom had given way to slump. By 1921 there was high unemployment and the edge was being taken off union militancy. Nevertheless, it seemed for a time that the miners' action would escalate into a general strike, as the railwaymen and transport workers backed the miners in their refusal to accept lower wages and local agreements.

All leave was stopped for members of the armed forces and the government declared a state of emergency. But Lloyd George was not resigned to a strike. On 14 April, Hodges, secretary of the miners' union, in a meeting with ministers at the House of Commons, compromised by implying that the miners might be prepared to forego their insistence on national rates, at least for a time. The following day Lloyd George seized on this opportunity, inviting the miners' leaders to a meeting to discuss a temporary settlement. But the miners' executive, which had not authorised Hodges' statement, repudiated their secretary and refused to attend. Hodges was a reasonable man, Lloyd George a very slippery one. Perhaps the Prime Minister realised that his invitation would drive a wedge between the miners and that the other two members of the triple alliance, who were becoming increasingly reluctant to take action, would be provided by this disunity with an excuse to avoid action. This was certainly the outcome.

On 15 April 1921, soon to be known as 'Black Friday', J.H. Thomas of the railwaymen's union abruptly cancelled support for the miners, and the transport workers did likewise. The 'triple alliance' had become the 'cripple alliance'. The miners went on strike alone and stayed out until 1 July, when they conceded defeat and returned to work on lower wages and with district agreements. They felt great bitterness towards their 'allies', who had let them down so badly by withdrawing support on a mere pretext. Thomas was, in his own words, subjected to 'abuse, calumny and misrepresentation'. In reality, the miners' two partners in the alliance had merely wanted to threaten a strike in order to get negotiations going: they had not actually wanted a strike. They knew that strike-breaking was much easier on the railways or in the docks than in the close-knit and often geographically isolated mining communities.

Union leaders did not forget 'Black Friday'. The miners decided that they could never again rely fully on their allies, while the other leaders were determined that they should never again be considered traitors. The incident left deep scars and affected trade unions until a general strike did take place in 1926.

Nevertheless, industrial relations improved after 1921. The severe slump of 1921–2 made unions more reluctant to strike, and the number of working days lost because of industrial action declined steadily from 1922 until 1925, in which year stoppages accounted for fewer than eight million days. The fact that inflation had given way to deflation added to this new economic industrial climate. Unions did not have to demand higher wages for their members: a higher standard of living would be secured automatically if wage rates were not cut. As a result, most disputes were caused by management attempts to secure wage cuts, leading not to 'strikes' (in which workers withdrew their labour) but to 'lock-outs' (in which owners closed factory gates until workers would accept cuts in their pay). Even the mines saw better industrial relations, and in 1924 the owners agreed to wage rises. In addition, Stanley Baldwin, Prime Minister from 1924 to 1929, was a man of goodwill who had the the sincere aim of promoting industrial peace. The omens for the future seemed bright.

3 The Origins of the General Strike

a) Wages and Conditions in the Mining Industry

Higher wages were conceded by the owners in 1924, but circumstances then were exceptional. There was a shortage of coal on the world market, and thus British coal was in demand and could command high prices. German coal was not available: the French had occupied the Ruhr in Germany in order to extract reparation payments in accordance with the Treaty of Versailles, and the Germans were responding with a campaign of passive resistance which effectively paralysed their coal industry. Strikes in the United States and Poland further enhanced the value of British coal. These conditions were unlikely to last long, and indeed in 1925 British coal again felt the full force of foreign competition. A new reparations deal with Germany, the Dawes Plan, meant that Germany paid her wartime debts by the export of free coal to France and Italy, whereupon the demand for British coal plummeted.

Nor were working conditions in British mines improved in the early 1920s. They were as poor as ever. Amenities such as pit-head baths were in short supply, and safety precautions were appalling, as can be judged by injury and death rates in the pits. A union official told the Sankey Commission that 'about four men are killed every 24 hours', and statistics collected between 1922 and 1924 largely bore out this statement. Over this three-year period 3,603 miners died and 597,193 were injured. These figures relate only to industrial accidents and do not take account of diseases, sometimes fatal, caused by the inhalation of coal dust over a long period. Anyone beginning work as a miner in 1920 would have a two per cent chance of being killed within the next 20 years, and a 50 per cent chance of being made seriously ill. Such casualty figures, which have been likened to those sustained in a war, are eloquent testimony explaining why industrial relations in the mining industry were so poor and why the industry was strike-prone. Mining was easily the most hazardous occupation in Britain, and many believed that in view of the dangers they ran the miners should at least be able to earn a living wage.

b) 'Red Friday'

As the price of coal fell on the world market, so profits for British coal owners began to decline. This, in turn, led the owners to seek lower costs of production. In 1925 the industry was running at a loss, and at the end of June 1925 the owners insisted on wage cuts and longer hours. The men judged that they were being asked to take pay cuts of between

13 and 48 per cent, while at the same time the owners were to retain their traditional rate of profit – indeed profits were to be guaranteed regardless of the price of coal. The miners would not accept these terms, and neither would their two national union leaders. The pliable Hodges had been replaced as secretary of the Miners' Federation by the fiery A.J. Cook, an ex-preacher who had been a syndicalist in the past (see page 38) and who was a member of the Communist Party. Beatrice Webb wrote that he was 'an inspired idiot' who became intoxicated with words when making a speech so that he scarcely knew what he had just said or was about to say next. The Federation's president, the Yorkshireman Herbert Smith, an orphan who had worked in the mines from the age of ten, was temperamentally very different. He was dour rather than emotional, a man of few words rather than a torrent. But both were incorruptible and devoted to the miners' cause.

The miners were prepared to fight alone. However, the General Council of the Trades Union Congress promised support, and a general strike once more seemed possible. Sympathetic action in support of the miners had failed to come about in April 1921, but TUC leaders had no wish to bear the stigma of another 'Black Friday'.

The government's reaction was to set up a court of inquiry under H.P. Macmillan. After their disillusioning experience with the Sankey Commission, the miners refused to co-operate; but the court nevertheless reported in their favour and against the owners, arguing that wages rather than profits should be the first charge on the industry. Baldwin saw representatives of the owners and of the unions separately but without achieving any breakthrough. Lower pay scales were to come into effect on 1 August 1925, at which time the TUC was to embargo the transportation of coal. Once more a general strike seemed almost certain.

Baldwin then acted. It can be argued that his government was in some degree responsible for the strike: by returning to the gold standard in April 1925, his Chancellor, Winston Churchill, had made British exports more expensive and therefore less competitive abroad (see page 104). No responsibility was admitted or acknowledged, but even so Baldwin intervened on 31 July and granted a subsidy to the coal industry so that wages and hours could remain at their existing level for nine months, while profits of up to 13 per cent would also be subsidised. In the meantime, a royal commission was to report on the industry and make recommendations on its future. Baldwin had defied the right wing of his party, whose members thought it disgraceful that taxpayers should subsidise any industry: the Prime Minister was said to have given way to union intimidation. The Home Secretary, Sir William Joynson-Hicks, believed the whole issue would have to be 'fought out'. Was the country, he asked, to be governed by a parliament 'or by a handful of trade union leaders'? The *Daily Mail* called it a 'victory for violence'.

Some have said that Baldwin was cynically buying time with the subsidy, postponing the strike until his government was better equipped to defeat it. Yet this seems unlikely for several reasons. First, as Cabinet papers reveal, the government was fairly confident of beating a strike in 1925. Second, Baldwin had a sincere faith in the possibility of industrial harmony and was a man of genuine goodwill. He had once said, of the Taff Vale judgement: 'The Conservatives can't talk of class war: they started it'. A general strike was really the last thing he wanted. His government was busy during the nine months of the subsidy, revising and improving existing plans for coping with a national strike, but this was not so much cynicism as practical politics. While hoping sincerely for the best, Baldwin had also to prepare for the worst.

As for the trade unions, they dubbed 31 July 'Red Friday'. Indeed some militants rejoiced in the belief that capitalism was failing: it almost seemed to them that a revolution was at hand. Most unionists thought that a great victory had been won. 'We have already beaten,' said Cook, 'not only the employers, but the strongest Government in modern times'. As a result of this optimism they made few preparations for a general strike, and so were at a decided disadvantage when one did occur.

c) The Samuel Report

Sir Herbert Samuel, a former Liberal home secretary, headed the royal commission. His report was ready in March 1926. It was a wide-ranging document and, though not calling for nationalisation, was highly critical of the whole mining industry. His recommendations contained much to displease the owners and to comfort the miners. The report called for the provision of pit-head baths and of decent houses at new collieries. It judged that wages should be agreed on a national basis, rather than local, and it also recommended that the working day should not be lengthened. This was currently seven hours, but working time began only when a miner reached the coalface, and this might be after walking or even crawling for a mile or two along narrow tunnels. (George Orwell, after personal experience, considered that 'this frightful business of crawling to and fro' was 'a hard day's work in itself'.) Samuel recommended that mining royalties should be nationalised, so that landowners would no longer receive profit for the coal mined by the companies, and called for the industry to be made more efficient by amalgamations. In addition, he wanted to see better retailing methods and more research into the uses to which coal could be put. Samuel believed that 'large progress' was possible along these lines, and he was adamant that no sacrifices should be required of the miners until the owners had agreed to adopt 'all practical means' for improving the organisation and efficiency of the industry.

Nevertheless, the report came to the conclusion that wage cuts were necessary in the short term. No precise level of reductions was specified, although Samuel implied that ten per cent might be sufficient. Only such cuts, it was argued, could save the industry from disaster. The report was in many ways an even-handed document, containing something for each side in the dispute, but on the crucial issue of wage cuts it came down against the unions. The vital question was whether the parties involved would now accept the report as the basis for a settlement.

d) The Failure of Negotiations

Negotiations began at a very leisurely pace. Representatives of the owners and the miners met two weeks after the publication of the Samuel report, and immediately there was deadlock. Neither side would accept the report's recommendations. The owners would not talk of reorganisation. Moreover they insisted on local as opposed to national wage agreements and still hankered after a longer working day. For their part, the union leaders would not accept wage cuts. Cook summed up the miners' position with the slogan 'not a penny off the pay, not a minute on the day'. Both Cook and Smith (whose most characteristic phrase was 'Nowt doin'') were poor negotiators, but the owners were also intransigent. There were some moderate and constructive owners, one of whom commented on the 'evil spirit' of one of his colleagues, but they were overshadowed by hard-liners. One government minister judged that he would describe the union leaders as 'the stupidest men in England' if he had not also met the owners! But perhaps the government should also be criticised. While trying to get the two sides together, Baldwin refused either to renew the subsidy or even to make recommendations of his own. He was advised by one moderate owner to 'force' or 'impose' a settlement on the owners, but this he refused to do. The owners then attempted to end the deadlock by imposing their own terms: they insisted on lower wages and a longer working day. When Smith and Cook rejected these terms, a lock-out began on Friday 30 April. The spectre of a general strike returned.

On 30 April 1926 almost 1,000 trade union representatives met in London and, after news reached them that the government had already proclaimed a state of emergency, they pledged support for the miners. Leading figures in the TUC had no positive wish for a strike: they tended to be much more moderate than Cook. This cleavage is best illustrated by the differences between Cook and J.H. Thomas, the railwaymen's leader and Labour MP. Cook was totally devoted to the miners' cause and had a contempt for the wealth of the capitalists. Thomas on the other hand, while retaining his proletarian image (so that he was said to drop his aitches as eagerly as he put on a dinner jacket), had acquired a taste for the 'good life' of high society. On the very day that Thomas was calling for 'a solution honourable and satisfactory to all sides', Cook was speaking of 'a war to the death'. Thomas warned his TUC colleagues that a general strike would lead to legislation against the unions and might indeed be a bloody affair in which their own lives would be in danger. Nevertheless the TUC felt that they must support the miners in their just cause.

It was agreed that a general strike should start at one minute past midnight on Tuesday 4 May. The miners' leaders then handed over 'the conduct of the dispute' to the General Council of the TUC and left London to help organise industrial action. Smith and Cook clearly believed at this stage that a general strike was inevitable; but in fact the TUC contacted the government again and began negotiating in earnest. The weekend was a very full and fraught one: ministers and TUC leaders had little sleep, so that tempers sometimes became frayed. At one time it seemed possible that the government would renew the subsidy for another fortnight in order for detailed negotiations to take place, but only on the precondition that the miners would agree in advance to accept some level of wage cuts. Miners' leaders were then recalled to the capital, but just as they returned the government broke off negotiations in the early hours of Monday 3 May. Baldwin had just heard that printers at the *Daily Mail* were refusing to work and, under pressure from the hard-liners in his Cabinet, decided that since industrial action had already begun further negotiations would be fruitless. TUC leaders were shocked, since they had neither authorised nor even known of the industrial action at the *Mail*. Having investigated the issue, they returned to Downing Street but were told that the Prime Minister had gone to bed.

e) Could the Negotiations Have Succeeded?

No one can be certain whether negotiations could have averted a strike: this is a highly controversial issue which has attracted contrasting verdicts from historians. However, it does seem that there were some grounds for a possible compromise. Cook was depicted in the press either as a dangerous revolutionary or as a short-sighted wishful-thinker unwilling to face economic reality (see the cartoons on pages 80 and 81). But there is evidence that he saw the need to compromise. He told one of Baldwin's secretaries (and therefore the Prime Minister himself) that the miners' position was so weak that 'we shall have to have a national minimum not only with pluses above it, but minuses below it'. Cook rarely expressed himself so clearly and too often indulged in anti-capitalist rhetoric, but even so a more adroit man than Baldwin might well have exploited this sign of flexibility.

The other possibility was that the TUC might have been detached from the miners, as on 'Black Friday'. Certainly J.H. Thomas had grave doubts about the wisdom of a general strike. The *Daily Mail*

Daily Herald, *28 July 1925*

incident was therefore of vital importance. One historian has judged that, without it, the moderates in the TUC would probably have called off their support of the miners. Certainly when the TUC delegates were told that the government was no longer willing to negotiate, General Secretary Citrine was not alone in feeling 'that we had not been treated fairly'.

The printers at the *Mail* had refused to print an inflammatory editorial which branded the proposed general strike an attempt to destroy the government and subvert the rights and liberties of the people. Their action was spontaneous and was not authorised by either the TUC or the printers' union. It was certainly not the case that the TUC had broken their word and begun the strike early. The govern-

Daily Graphic, *28 April 1926*

ment side may therefore have used the action as an excuse to break off
negotiations, and for this they should be criticised. It has even been
suggested that Churchill, who had visited the offices of the *Daily Mail*
earlier that day, might have arranged for the editorial to be written in
the hope of provoking just such a reaction. The case against the
Chancellor is not proven, but he certainly responded to the news with
vigour: 'A great organ of the press is muzzled by strikers'. A colleague
described him at this point as 'getting frantic with excitement and
eagerness to begin the battle'.

f) Causes of the General Strike: an Overview

The strike had a remarkably long fuse, so that its origins can be traced back several generations. It may be seen as the culmination of a long history of bitter industrial relations in the mines, which in turn may be traced to poor working conditions, an appalling accident rate, and the failure of the owners to produce a coherent and efficient structure for the industry. Another mining dispute was nothing out of the ordinary and thus in a sense does not need explaining: the problems of the industry, exposed by successive reports but never rectified, meant that further industrial confrontation was only to be expected.

It is therefore important to distinguish between the causes of the mining dispute of 1926 and those of the sympathetic action authorised by the TUC. It was the latter which transformed yet another mining dispute into the unique General Strike. TUC action owed much to feelings of guilt at the withdrawal of support on 'Black Friday' and to the widespread belief that, though economic realities demanded some reduction in wages, the owners were treating the men unfairly. Samuel later said that his commissioners never even contemplated such severe reductions in pay as the owners were seeking to impose. The TUC was also motivated by the need for solidarity in the face of the threat that, if miners' wages were reduced, general pay reductions for British workers might well follow. In 1925, during negotiations, Baldwin had said that 'all the workers of this country have got to take a reduction of wages to help put industry on its feet'. Self-interest thus seemed to unite all workers in a common struggle. Nevertheless, the reluctance of the TUC to take action must be emphasised: they sincerely wanted to find a way to avoid confrontation, and ideally they wanted to achieve a solution by the threat rather than the reality of common action. In the end it was the government which gave them little choice but to go through with the first general strike in British history.

Responsibility for the strike must be shared between four groups: the miners' leaders, the TUC, the coal owners and the government. All these parties believed they were victims, but none can escape some share of the blame. Miners' leaders failed to convince their members that some wage cuts were necessary. The TUC representatives allowed themselves to drift into the position of entering a strike of which they disapproved. The colliery owners adopted an extreme position and refused compromise. Baldwin's government did little to bring the two sides together and called off negotiations when there was still a slight chance of averting the strike. The origins of the General Strike constitute a story with no heroes and with several parties contending for the role of villains.

4 The General Strike, 4–12 May 1926

a) The TUC and the Strike

Already one million miners were on strike (or, rather, were locked out). Now, on 4 May, the TUC called out the railwaymen, dockers, road transport workers, printers, and gas and electricity workers. Engineering and shipbuilding workers were asked to strike a week later. In all, some 80 unions were affected and about two and a half million men and women went on strike, in addition to the miners. The response to the strike call was not uniform throughout the country. Some seamen resolutely stayed at work, and some parts of the countryside were very little affected. But what is really remarkable about the strike is the degree of worker solidarity that *was* shown. For instance, even at the end of the strike well over 90 per cent of railwaymen were solid in their refusal to work. There was very little sign of a drift back to work as the strike proceeded. It was, in fact, the most complete stoppage in Britain's history.

However, the TUC did not call for a universal strike. Workers in the health and sanitary services were excluded from the strike call, as were those who transported food, although the government refused the TUC's offer of maintaining food distribution. It was also hoped – naively – that power workers, while cutting off the supply of heat, would be able to maintain lighting. Nor was the term 'general strike', with its syndicalist and revolutionary overtones, favoured by the TUC: instead, they used the phrase 'national strike'. Having entered the strike very reluctantly, the General Council was anxious to show that it was not revolutionary and that it was involved in an industrial rather than a political dispute. Hence it tried to pursue 'moderate' policies, especially by attempting to minimise the inconvenience to the general public. The General Council also tried to make the strike appear as respectable as possible. For this reason it declined a donation to the strike fund of two million roubles (around £26,000) from Russian trade unions. Citrine even went to the trouble of obtaining police permission before sending half a dozen men to picket the offices of *The Times*, and there was no attempt to use mass picketing or intimidation anywhere. Strikers were advised to stay at home, or to dig the garden, rather than to go out on the streets. Approval was given to sporting contests, and the TUC hoped that a football match at Plymouth between strikers and the police (won by the former by two goals to one) would symbolise the essentially moderate nature of the strike.

The TUC's direction of the strike was hindered by lack of effective preparations. It was due to the administrative skills and hard work of Ernest Bevin (a man who negotiated a 44-hour working week for the dockers but worked an 80-hour week himself) that some sort of coherence was improvised. However, there was still a good deal of muddle. The local strike committees which were set up in towns and cities often received ambiguous instructions – or none at all – from TUC headquarters. Indeed the Swansea committee was so confused by contradictory messages that its members began to suspect that these constituted misinformation deliberately sent by the government. In this case the committee was wrong, but the government did intercept telegrams to and from the TUC and tap telephone lines.

The main worry of the union leaders was that their inability fully to control the strike throughout the country might allow violence to erupt. The popular image that has survived of the General Strike is of its good-humoured holiday atmosphere. But this is a misleading half-truth. Certainly there were some worrying moments. Buses were overturned in Glasgow, police baton-charged crowds in Doncaster, and there were numerous other incidents, including some hand-to-hand fighting that looked as though it might turn vicious. Nevertheless, such incidents were 'rumblings before a storm that never broke'. Over 3,000 people (including prominent members of strike committees) were arrested and prosecuted, but given that the strike involved millions of people this figure is remarkably small. The longest prison sentence meted out was eight years, for someone who had helped derail an express train, the *Flying Scotsman*: the driver had in fact been stopped and warned that the rails had been pulled up, but he chose to drive on. Luckily no one was seriously injured in this incident. Nevertheless the TUC was anxious. Because authority was never fully in the hands of the General Council, it might pass to the local strike committees, which some called 'embryo soviets' on the Russian model. Certainly it seemed that the longer the strike went on, the greater was the likelihood that the TUC would lose control.

b) The Government and the Strike

While the TUC was anxious to appear moderate, the government was much more provocative. Almost its first action was to brand the strike a challenge to the constitution, rather than an attempt to stop the exploitation of the miners. This was the message printed in the government's newspaper, the *British Gazette*. Baldwin appointed Churchill as its editor ('the cleverest thing I ever did: otherwise he'd have wanted to shoot someone'), and soon its circulation reached two million copies. There was no attempt at impartial journalism. Churchill said he could not be impartial 'as between the fire brigade and the fire'. He used the paper as a weapon in a propaganda war with the TUC, which replied with its own *British Worker*.

On 6 May the *Gazette* printed the following editorial:

1 The General Strike is in operation, expressing in no uncertain terms a direct challenge to ordered government. It would be futile

to attempt to minimise the seriousness of such a challenge, constituting as it does an effort to force upon some 42,000,000
5 British citizens the will of less than 4,000,000 others engaged in the vital services of the country.

The strike is intended as a direct hold-up of the nation to ransom. It is for the nation to stand firm in its determination not to flinch. 'This moment,' as the Prime Minister pointed out in the
10 House of Commons, 'has been chosen to challenge the existing Constitution of the country and to substitute the reign of force for that which now exists . . . I do not think all the leaders who assented to order a general strike fully realised that they were threatening the basis of ordered government and coming nearer to
15 proclaiming civil war than we have been for centuries past'.

The following day came the response of the General Council of the TUC in the *British Worker*:

1 The General Council does not challenge the Constitution. It is not seeking to substitute unconstitutional government. Nor is it desirous of undermining our Parliamentary institutions. The sole aim of the Council is to secure for the miners a decent standard of
5 life. The Council is engaged in an Industrial Dispute . . . Every instruction issued by the General Council is evidence of their determination to maintain the struggle strictly on the basis of an industrial dispute. They have ordered every member taking part to be exemplary in his conduct and not to give any cause for police
10 interference. The General Council struggled hard for peace. They are anxious that an honourable peace shall be secured as soon as possible. They are not attacking the Constitution. They are not fighting the community. They are defending the mine workers against the mine owners.

Many judged that Churchill won this war of propaganda, for however moderate the TUC leaders might be during the strike and however much they might protest that they were merely supporting the miners in a just cause, the fact was that their action was designed to coerce not the owners but the government. It was easy, therefore, to present the General Strike primarily as a contest between an elected government and a trade union organisation that did not represent the mass of the people. The fundamental issue tended to be seen as 'Under Which Flag?' (see the cartoon on page 86).

Churchill skilfully simplified the issues involved in the strike and called for the 'unconditional surrender' of the strikers. He also spread misleading information, insisting that strikers in particular parts of the country were returning to work when in fact they were not. Furthermore, when the government recruited a quarter of a million special

UNDER WHICH FLAG?

JOHN BULL. ' ONE OF THESE TWO FLAGS HAS GOT TO COME DOWN—AND IT WON'T BE MINE."

Punch *cartoon, 12 May 1926*

constables – many armed with chair legs because regulation truncheons were in short supply – Churchill insisted provocatively that 'any action they may find it necessary to take' would have the full support of the government. The King himself found it necessary to complain about this, insisting that the law of the land should govern the conduct of all.

The government's plans, laid before the strike, worked well during it. The country had been divided into ten areas, each under a civil commissioner, and essential services were maintained. Troops were used to man power stations, and there was no shortage of volunteers to help out. The government recruited men and women, and a private organisation, the 'Organisation for the Maintenance of Supplies', also put itself at the government's disposal. The unions believed that members of fascist organisations acted as volunteers and did their best to foment trouble. Certainly, several volunteers asked to be sent to Glasgow, where they could 'have a crack at them dirty Bolshies on the Clyde'. However, most volunteers probably joined for the fun of novel work. Some fulfilled a lifetime's ambition to drive a train. Many undergraduates took part, the overwhelming number on the government's side, and members of the House of Lords were also eager to participate: three served as an engine-driver, a guard and a station-master. A former foreign secretary, Lord Grey, who was nearly blind, said he could not work as a special constable because he might hit the wrong man on the nose, but he was determined to unload ships. Such was the lack of expertise among the volunteers that many accidents occurred, especially on the railways, where four people were killed and at least 35 injured. One man even contrived to drive a tram off its rails.

c) The End of the Strike

Baldwin broadcast to the nation on 8 May. He insisted that while he could not negotiate until the strike had been called off, he was nevertheless a man who was 'longing and working and praying for peace'. He asked to be trusted to 'secure even justice between man and man'. On the same day, in sharp contrast, he and his Cabinet approved a bill that was to declare sympathetic strike action illegal, forbid picketing and make trade union funds liable for damages. It was decided that, unless the strike ended quickly, the bill would be pushed through Parliament in a single day. But there were signs that the legislation would not be needed. Certainly Baldwin's skilful words on the radio, confirming his reputation as a moderate, made a real appeal to the TUC. By this time the General Council was beginning to regret calling the strike in the first place. There were few signs that worker solidarity was crumbling: indeed Bevin said that anyone suggesting in the East End of London that the strike should be ended 'would be in danger of his life'. But neither was there any sign that the strike would achieve an early victory. It looked as though it might be a long contest:

and the longer it went on the greater were the chances that violence might flare up and the initiative pass to the revolutionaries. Several observers at this time independently drew parallels with the Russian Revolution, where the moderate Kerensky had been quickly replaced by Lenin.

The TUC was dismayed by an opinion voiced in Parliament on 5 May by the Liberal lawyer Sir John Simon that a general strike was already illegal – an incorrect verdict but one reiterated by a judge a few days later – and that therefore trade union assets might be seized. Thomas, the most reluctant member of the General Council to accept the strike in the first place, was the foremost voice in favour of ending it. He himself had organised several railway strikes in the past, but the longest had been of only ten days' duration. Acutely aware that, unlike the mines, railways were not 'blackleg-proof', he insisted that the government was bound to win and that the longer the strike went on the more needless hardship would be caused. Thomas was therefore pleased when he was contacted by Sir Herbert Samuel, who had recently returned from a holiday in Italy and put himself forward as mediator.

Samuel proposed a brief renewal of the subsidy, a return to work at the old rates of pay and then the resumption of negotiations to decide on reorganisation and wage reductions. Thomas seized on this initiative, even though Samuel made it quite clear that his proposals had not been accepted by the government. Joint talks were held on 10 and 11 May between Samuel, the General Council and the miners' leaders. Smith and Cook were not told that Samuel spoke without government approval, but even so there was no agreement. The TUC was for calling off the strike on the Samuel formula, but the miners were against. The miners, aggrieved that talks had started without their knowledge, would not agree in advance that wages should be cut. There was deadlock and an increasing bitterness between the TUC and the miners' leaders.

Walter Citrine's diary for 11 May is revealing of TUC thinking:

1   . . . reports came in from the country and showed that the men
    are as firm as a rock. What then can be the cause of apprehension?
    I think it is because most of us know that no matter how
    determined our men are now, once the strike has reached its
5   highest point and the maximum of members have been called out,
    a gradual decline in economic power must ensue. Then we shall
    have dribblings back to work here and there . . .
       Our Council have quickly come to the view that they must
    make their own decision in respect of policy.
10 Today Bevin said: 'I am not concerned what the miners may
    think about it. They can say what they like about me. My union
    came into this business on very definite terms, and I have told my
    men so. The dockers will stick out for weeks, and so will the

miners, but I don't think it is right to go on asking men to make
15 sacrifices if we can get justice any other way. The other side does
not want to fight this matter out to a finish'.
  Thomas assented readily. 'I don't think so either. Some of
them do, but the business men don't.'
  ... Herbert Smith is immovable. Some of our Council mem-
20 bers think he does not care who goes down. He will not give in.

The breach between the TUC and the miners was now seemingly
unbridgeable. Memories of 'Black Friday' no longer had much effect on
the General Council, one of whose members mused that 'Judas Iscariot
played a dramatic part in history. There could have been no Jesus
Christ without him'. Another said that they should 'no longer grovel on
our hands and knees before the miners'.
  On 12 May the General Council announced the ending of their
sympathetic action. The government had made it clear to Samuel that
his proposals were 'not clothed in even a vestige of official character',
and they were categorically determined not to resume the subsidy. The
TUC had therefore surrendered unconditionally, even though they
never admitted it to themselves. Many strikers were joyful when they
heard the news that the strike was over – they assumed that they must
have won. It therefore came as a bitter shock to realise that the TUC
had capitulated. The Communist Party described the calling off of the
strike as 'the greatest crime that has ever been committed'. Another
observer described the unions as 'an army of lions led by a few
jackasses'.
  TUC leaders had hoped that Baldwin would first use his influence to
ensure that no returning strikers suffered victimisation from employers, and would then help to solve the mining dispute on the basis of
Samuel's proposals. But they had obtained no assurances, and in fact
the Prime Minister did nothing of the kind. Some returning strikers
faced dismissal and many more faced reduced wages. The result was
that, on 13 May, a second – and spontaneous – strike began in protest.
Indeed it is probable that more people refused to work after the strike
had been called off than during the nine days of the official strike. Most
employers then became more flexible, but even so it is probable that
many thousands were victimised in some way as a result of their
support for the General Strike.
  As for the miners, they reaped no benefit from the massive sympathetic action launched by the TUC. Chancellor of the Exchequer Winston
Churchill tried hard to achieve a settlement, and to force the owners to
compromise, but without success. The miners stayed on strike until the
end of the year but finally had to admit total defeat – reduced wages,
longer hours and local wage agreements. Even their unity was dam-
aged, as a breakaway 'non-political' union was formed in Nottingham-
shire.

d) Why the Strike Failed

The General Strike, literally a 'nine days' wonder', achieved greater support from workers and their families than even optimistic union leaders had predicted. A cabinet minister wrote in his diary that 'immense numbers of workers' had come out against their will and were 'longing to go back', but were afraid to be so because of fear that their families would be bullied. However, there is little evidence to support this view. The strike exhibited remarkable worker solidarity and cannot be said to have collapsed. So why did it fail?

One important factor was that the government had planned well for the strike. The civil servant who masterminded its plans, Sir John Anderson, had done so with remarkable thoroughness. 'Before the computer was perfected,' it has been said, 'Anderson was a tolerable substitute'. In sharp contrast, the unions had failed to plan at all for the strike. After 'Red Friday', they had judged the battle already won. A.J. Cook, for instance, merely advised his mother-in-law to buy an extra tin of salmon each week – drawing from J.H. Thomas the caustic comment 'By God! A British revolution based on a tin of salmon'.

Another vital factor in the failure of the strike was the readiness of people to act as 'patriotic volunteers' (from the point of view of the government) or 'strike breakers and blacklegs' (from the standpoint of the unions). The railways were virtually paralysed, despite the efforts of the volunteers, but road transport functioned relatively smoothly and prevented the strike from having maximum impact. In earlier decades, before the proliferation of motor vehicles, the strike would have been much more effective.

These factors meant that the strike could not succeed in the short term – a crucial fact, since the TUC were banking on a quick victory. The General Council were not revolutionaries: they were responsible and moderate men, anxious that the strides made by trade unionists over the previous decades should not be destroyed. They were reluctant to take sympathetic action in the first place and had no wish to see the strike produce bitter and violent confrontation.

The TUC leaders were caught in a logical dilemma which, in the end, almost guaranteed their defeat. They authorised strike action to support the miners in their battle to prevent a 'savage deterioration' in their living conditions. In this sense the strike was an industrial dispute. However, their sympathetic action was designed to coerce not the mine owners but the government, and as a result politicians were able to present the action as a challenge to the constitution. In this sense the General Strike was political. In the resulting battle of words, which put the unions on the defensive, the miners' cause was pushed into the background. Perhaps the TUC would have done better not to call out the printers, since by this action it allowed the government, through control of the *British Gazette* and the BBC, to achieve a stranglehold over the media which the improvised *British Worker* could do little to loosen. Soon it seemed to the TUC that they had everything to lose from the strike and nothing to gain. At this stage Samuel's intervention provided them with a convenient pretext to call off an action which, all along, their heads had told them was unwise.

The TUC leaders have been heavily criticised. They have been called timid men who mistrusted their supporters more than their opponents and who feared the consequences of victory more than those of defeat. They were not 'consciously traitorous', one historian has written, 'but they lacked moral fibre'. Thomas, in particular, has been the butt of criticism: there were 'mules and fools' among the strike leaders, but only one traitor. On the other hand, it can be argued that the General Council's reasoning was correct: the strike was not being won, union funds were being exhausted in strike pay, and sooner or later violence might have spread. Much depends on the hypothetical issue of what would have occurred had the strike continued; but it is at least arguable that the TUC were acting sensibly in calling it off. Perhaps if the miners' representatives had been more shrewd then they too would have ended the strike on 12 May. Certainly they achieved absolutely nothing by staying out for another seven months, and pitiful reports of hardship in mining communities – with women about to give birth without adequate food, clothing or bedding – show the price they paid.

The miners had been able to call on the TUC as their allies, but this escalation of the dispute enabled the mine owners to call on the government. It was an unequal contest. The General Strike failed because the TUC was opposed by the resolute power of the government and of the State. Baldwin, stiffened by his right wing, could not allow the strike to succeed. Detachments of the British army were stationed outside many of the major cities. Their use was not authorised, but it would have been had the situation deteriorated. The State could also call on vast financial resources. The nine-month coal subsidy, which Baldwin had been so reluctant to renew, totalled £23 million; but in the nine days of the strike the government spent a total of £433 million. In contrast the trade unions spent £4 million and could afford no more.

e) Significance of the Strike

How should the General Strike be interpreted? There are two basic issues – what the strike tells us about industrial relations between 1919 and 1926, and its effects on the future.

One school of thought emphasises that the strike was really about class warfare. According to this interpretation, leaders on the left had long been dreaming of a general strike to bring about a fundamental shift in political power, while capitalists and right-wing politicians such as Churchill and Joynson-Hicks had long been aiming to crush the trade union movement and reassert the power of property-owners. This antagonism came to a head in 1926. There is some truth in this analysis: the events of 1926 reveal much class solidarity – for instance, the volunteers were almost all middle-class – together with hostility and antagonism between classes, and certainly there were leading figures on both left and right with extreme and belligerent attitudes. The problem with this line of argument is that such men were less important in 1926 than is often imagined. Cook had certainly been a syndicalist in his earlier years, but his biographer has shown that by 1926 he was no longer a revolutionary: he wished merely to defend the miners' position and was far from optimistic about the outcome. In the end, he simply bowed to the wishes of the majority of miners. On the government side, Baldwin did much to tame his right wing, and even Churchill, who was so provocative during the strike, proved remarkably conciliatory after it. Nor did employers conform to type: they reduced wages in the wake of the strike less markedly than they had in the period before it (perhaps a sign that the strike was not altogether a failure). It seems fair to conclude, therefore, that the General Strike was not the result only of class antagonism but also of specific problems and, to some degree, of the mistakes and miscalculations of individuals. It is not difficult to imagine that, had the adroit Lloyd George rather than the stolid Stanley Baldwin been Prime Minister, a general strike might well have been averted.

Nor was the General Strike necessarily the climax of industrial bitterness in the period after the First World War. It can be argued that 1919–21 saw the height of militancy, with a crop of unofficial strikes, political demands from Labour and a record number of working days lost. 1922–5, a period of relatively high unemployment, saw a lessening of industrial conflict and fewer days lost. The events of 1926 were perhaps merely an exception to the broad trend of better industrial relations.

What of the effects of the General Strike? Was the strike a turning point? Such a dramatic event as Britain's first and (so far) only General Strike must, it is assumed, have had clear-cut and momentous consequences. The commonest interpretation is that the strike was both an end and a beginning – an end to the old romantic notions of syndicalism and direct action and the beginning of a new mood which stressed moderation and collaboration in trade union affairs. Historians generally have a liking for clear-cut interpretations, but sometimes historical reality is so complex as to defy such simple analysis. There was admittedly a trend towards moderation after 1926, but under men like Bevin and Thomas this had been apparent even earlier, and the General Strike was not the only factor making for collaboration between capital and labour. High unemployment levels after 1926, and in particular during the depression of 1929–32, were also important. Nor should it be supposed that no one on the left henceforth hankered after revolution. The General Strike was seen by some hard-liners as a magnificent demonstration of working-class power that would have achieved victory but for its betrayal by spineless TUC leaders. 'The response of the workers was beyond all praise', wrote the *Workers' Weekly*, but 'the leadership was beyond contempt'. The mystique of a general strike had thus not been entirely destroyed. There was both change and continuity after 1926.

5 Industrial Relations, 1927–39

a) The Trade Disputes Act, 1927

After the General Strike, Baldwin found it impossible to resist calls from right-wingers for a change in the law. The Trade Disputes Act was the result. It made any strike illegal that was 'designed or calculated to coerce the Government either directly or by inflicting hardship upon the community'. There could be no repetition of May 1926. Strike activity had to be confined to the 'trade or industry in which the strikers are engaged'. Illegal 'intimidation' during strikes was defined more widely than ever before. Finally, the Act insisted that henceforth trade unionists who wanted to pay the political levy to the Labour Party would have to make a point of 'contracting in'. Before this all unionists had paid unless they deliberately 'contracted out'. Because of the apathy of many workers, who had not troubled to contract out before 1927 and did not trouble to contract in afterwards, Labour Party funds soon declined significantly; but if the government hoped to weaken the links between Labour and the unions it signally failed. The unions now rallied behind Labour, as they had done after Taff Vale, in an effort to secure change through Parliament and especially to get the 1927 Act repealed.

b) The Mond–Turner Talks

There was a good deal of bitterness from rank and file union members towards their leaders after May 1926, but it soon subsided. Almost all the leaders of 1926 were re-elected to their offices. Most union members decided that the whole episode of the General Strike – and not just its ending – had been a mistake. A new temper in industrial relations gradually became apparent.

In 1928 and 1929 a series of meetings took place between employers and the TUC. These talks were named after Sir Alfred Mond, a moderate coal-owner and the creator of Imperial Chemical Industries, and Ben Turner, Chairman of the TUC. But the two key individuals were Mond and Ernest Bevin, both of whom believed that employers and workers should co-operate out of enlightened self-interest. Cook, disgusted at this dialogue with the industrial enemy, cast scorn on 'Mond Moonshine', and it must be admitted that little of practical benefit emerged from the talks. A joint report recommended changes in industry to the benefit of both employers and workers – and especially regular consultations between management and unions in each industry – but the depression beginning in 1929 provided poor circumstances for the implementation of reforms. The talks may have helped the General Council to recover some prestige after the General Strike, but on the whole they symbolised the new industrial atmosphere rather than achieved concrete improvements in industrial relations.

c) Effects of the Great Depression

The Great Depression lasted from 1929 to 1932. Unemployment peaked at three million, but even after this period parts of British industry were heavily depressed (see page 55). As a consequence, union membership – and therefore union revenue – declined. Membership totals fell from a maximum of over eight million in 1921 to a low point of 4,392,000 (less than one-third of all wage earners) in 1934. Even so, these figures should be seen in perspective. The blows trade unionism suffered put the clock back, but only to the position of 1914. Union membership at its lowest point in the 1930s was still four times the size of that in 1888, and from 1934 onwards there was expansion. In 1939 just over six million workers were in trade unions.

During the depression industrial relations were undoubtedly strained. Collaboration between unions had been dealt a blow by the General Strike, but even so national strikes took place in the textile industry in 1929, 1930, 1931 and 1932. Nevertheless conditions did not favour strikers – too many firms were going bankrupt and too many unemployed workers were willing to act as strike-breakers – and the decade has been described as one of 'sullen industrial peace'. Indeed between 1927 and 1939 the average annual total of working days lost was just over three million, compared with 28 million between 1919 and 1925. In 1934, for instance, fewer working days (a mere 959,000) were lost in strikes than in any year since 1900. Rather than take the offensive, most union leaders simply tried to minimise wage-cutting. Even the mines were relatively peaceful. Smith retired as president of the miners' union in 1930 and Cook died the following year. They were replaced by more moderate figures.

Ernest Bevin, the leader of Britain's largest union (the TGWU) and Chairman of the General Council of the TUC in 1936–7, was the key figure in this period. His biographer has described him as 'the outstanding trade-union leader yet produced by this, or perhaps any other, country'. He worked extremely well with Walter Citrine, the General Secretary of the TUC, even though the two men were of contrasting temperaments and indeed disliked each other. It has been said that they formed 'one of the most successful involuntary partnerships in modern politics'. Under their leadership, the TUC became much stronger than ever before. The 'Bridlington Agreement' of 1939 enabled the TUC to settle disputes between unions and laid down precise regulations to govern union competition and to prevent the poaching of members. The General Council also assumed the power to expel offending unions.

Bevin also helped to hammer out a series of policies in the 1930s which, it was believed, would combat depression and spearhead economic growth. Trade unions had become much more politically-minded than ever before, and much more constructive. Tariffs, assisted emigration and public works were all recommended. It is generally agreed that the TUC had far more progressive ideas at this time than did the official Labour Party. TUC leaders were converted 'to Keynes rather than Marx' (see page 114). Even Conservative politicians now listened to what the unions had to say, and in 1937 Bevin claimed that the unions were an integral part of the State. Certainly their officials found numerous positions on governmental advisory committees and commissions. Bevin himself sat on a committee which extended the benefits of an annual holiday with pay to an extra eight million workers. But, despite this, his claim was perhaps premature. It was during the Second World War, as in the war of 1914–18, that the unions were taken into partnership with government. By 1940, when Bevin became Minister of Labour and National Service, history had indeed come full circle, and the General Strike had been forgotten by all but a few.

Making notes on 'The General Strike and Industrial Relations Between the Wars'

The headings and sub-headings used in the text should help you to make effective notes on this chapter. You will need most details on the General Strike itself. As well as (i) making a summary of the economic pre-conditions of the strike, (ii) describing the main individuals concerned, (iii) making a narrative of events and (iv) summarising the results of the strike, you should focus on two issues: the causes of the strike and the reasons for its failure. Hence you should pause at sections 3(f) and 4(d) and try to evaluate the importance of the various factors involved. No consensus has emerged about the roles of the owners, the miners' leaders and the TUC leaders or the responsibility the government should bear, and therefore we must all make up our own minds. To ensure that you fully consider both sides of each issue, you might try first to sympathise with and then to criticise each of these groups, before coming to your own conclusion.

Alternatively, you could compile your notes in a more ambitious way. Take the three key questions 'Why did the General Strike start?',

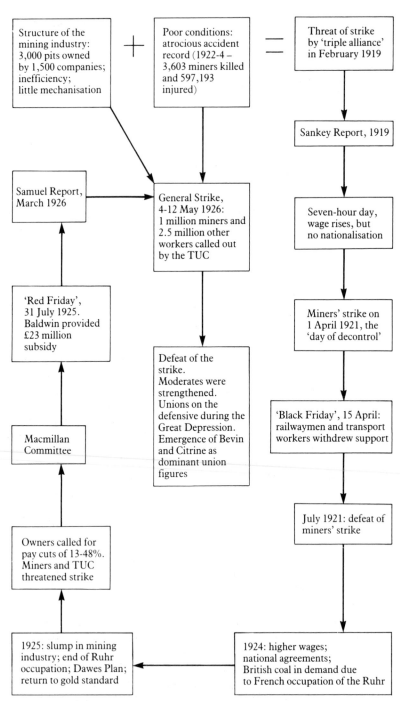

| Structure of the mining industry: 3,000 pits owned by 1,500 companies; inefficiency; little mechanisation | + | Poor conditions: atrocious accident record (1922-4 – 3,603 miners killed and 597,193 injured) | = | Threat of strike by 'triple alliance' in February 1919 |

Sankey Report, 1919

Samuel Report, March 1926

General Strike, 4-12 May 1926: 1 million miners and 2.5 million other workers called out by the TUC

Seven-hour day, wage rises, but no nationalisation

'Red Friday', 31 July 1925. Baldwin provided £23 million subsidy

Miners' strike on 1 April 1921, the 'day of decontrol'

Defeat of the strike. Moderates were strengthened. Unions on the defensive during the Great Depression. Emergence of Bevin and Citrine as dominant union figures

Macmillan Committee

'Black Friday', 15 April: railwaymen and transport workers withdrew support

Owners called for pay cuts of 13-48%. Miners and TUC threatened strike

July 1921: defeat of miners' strike

1925: slump in mining industry; end of Ruhr occupation; Dawes Plan; return to gold standard

1924: higher wages; national agreements; British coal in demand due to French occupation of the Ruhr

Summary – The General Strike and Industrial Relations Between the Wars

'Why did the General Strike fail?' and 'What were the results of the General Strike?', and try to construct your notes as an answer to them. Only attempt to give this structure to your notes if you feel confident that you have thoroughly understood the contents of the chapter.

Answering essay questions on 'The General Strike and Industrial Relations Between the Wars'

Essay questions on the General Strike are common. They can either single out the strike itself or consider it as part of a longer time-span.

1 Discuss the view that the General Strike was doomed to failure from the start.
2 Why did the General Strike fail and what were the consequences of this failure for the future?
3 Why were industrial relations issues so important in British politics between 1918 and 1927?

It is worth spending some time thinking about these questions. (Question 2 is unsatisfactory in that you are not told whether each section of the question carries equal marks, though it is probably best to work on this assumption.) Construct both first and final paragraphs for all three questions, being careful to avoid repetition. Remember that while at the start of an essay you may *outline* an argument, in the conclusion you must be much more precise. For instance, for the third question, while you might in the first paragraph voice various possible explanations for the importance of industrial relations issues, by the final paragraph you should be much more definite, perhaps by high-lighting the most important factor. Try a 'brainstorming' session to identify half a dozen possible alternative reasons.

Alternatively, questions can focus on a longer period of time. For example:

4 What factors affected the development of the trade union move-ment between 1914 and 1927?
5 How powerful was the trade union movement between 1918 and 1939?

The first question is relatively straightforward. Construct a list of 'factors'. Such an exercise will go a long way towards answering the question, but how will you frame your essay so as avoid it appearing like a list? What overall argument will you give? How will you approach question 5? Clearly you must break your answer down into particular periods – which ones? What are the yardsticks for assessing trade union power? How much emphasis will you give to membership totals, as compared with successful strike action or the position of trade unions in the law?

Sourced based questions on 'The General Strike and Industrial Relations Between the Wars'

1 Cartoons of A.J. Cook
Study the cartoons on pages 80 and 81, from the *Daily Herald* and the *Daily Graphic*. Answer the following questions:
a) The *Herald* cartoon is dated 28 July 1925 and the *Graphic* cartoon 28 April 1926. What events prompted them? Explain which depiction you think more accurately reflects Cook's role in those events. *(6 marks)*
b) Comment on the way the *Herald*'s cartoonist has drawn Cook. Is he being criticised or praised? Justify your answer. *(4 marks)*
c) Comment on the way the cartoonist has drawn Cook in the *Graphic*. What impression of him would the reader gain? *(5 marks)*

2 Citrine's diary
Read the extracts from Walter Citrine's diary for 11 May on page 88. Answer the following questions:
a) How close to favouring the calling off of the strike do you think Citrine was, given the first paragraph of this extract? Explain your answer. *(4 marks)*
b) What did Citrine mean by saying that the Council were to make 'their own decision in respect of policy' (line 9)? What were the implications of this statement? *(5 marks)*
c) What might Bevin have meant by saying that his union 'came into this business on very definite terms' (line 12)? *(3 marks)*
d) How would you characterise the mood of this meeting, as described by Citrine? Justify your answer. *(3 marks)*

3 Newspapers during the General Strike
Read the extracts from the *British Gazette* and the *British Worker* on pages 84–5. Answer the following questions:
a) Churchill insisted in the *Gazette* that four million strikers were challenging 42 million citizens. Given that Britain's total population was around 46 million, can these figures be justified? Explain your answer. *(3 marks)*
b) Was Churchill justified in calling the strike 'a direct hold-up of the nation to ransom' (line 7)? Explain your answer. *(4 marks)*
c) Baldwin had a reputation for being a moderate. How far is this

reputation borne out by his statement to the House of Commons (lines 9–15 in the *Gazette*)? *(3 marks)*

d) What, in practical terms, do you think the author of the *British Worker* extract meant by i) 'a decent standard of life for the miners' (line 4), and ii) 'an honourable peace' (line 11)? *(4 marks)*

e) Are there any signs in the extract from the *British Worker* that the TUC's willingness to continue the strike was faltering? Support your answer with quotations from the extract. *(3 marks)*

f) Compare and contrast the two extracts as pieces of propaganda. *(8 marks)*

4 'Under Which Flag?'

Study the *Punch* cartoon of 12 May 1926 on page 86. Answer the following questions:

a) How effectively does the cartoon summarise the main issues at stake in the General Strike? *(5 marks)*

b) What is the cartoonist attempting to communicate to his audience in his depiction of John Bull (the traditional symbol of Britain)? Explain your answer in detail. *(5 marks)*

c) Comment on the TUC representative so as to illustrate the impression that the cartoonist was trying to give of the trade union movement. *(5 marks)*

d) What do you think is the political message of the cartoon? Support your answer in detail. *(5 marks)*

CHAPTER 6

Governments and the Economy

1 The Treasury View and the Return to Gold, 1918–25

a) Post-war Boom and Bust, 1918–22

Lloyd George won a general election at the end of 1918 with a promise to create 'homes fit for heroes'. There was a general expectation that governments would intervene much more actively in the economy than before the war in order to promote the welfare of British citizens. The Minister of Reconstruction voiced a widely-held view in 1918 when he said that the war through which the country had passed 'has enlarged its sense of what is possible, and at the same time quickened its sense of what is fair and right'. The economy had been mobilised for war and now, it seemed, it would be mobilised to ensure higher standards of living in peacetime.

Before the war Lloyd George had introduced old age pensions and national insurance against sickness and unemployment. Now he not only extended the insurance system to include allowances for dependants of the unemployed but also began an ambitious house-building programme. As during the war, he showed a bold willingness to improvise and to innovate. In 1921 he chose Sir Robert Horne, the candidate he described as the 'least wedded to financial orthodoxy', as his Chancellor of the Exchequer. Yet in the circumstances of 1921, when the post-war boom ended (see page 49), not even the new Chancellor could resist traditional policies. Lloyd George's coalition was dependent on the support of the Conservative Party, and Tory MPs insisted that since government revenue was falling – with fewer people in work and so able to pay tax – government expenditure should be cut back. In 1922 the 'Geddes' Axe', wielded by a Tory minister, pruned expenditure by over ten per cent. Here was an end to the government's radical policies. The last wartime controls were removed and the housing programme was abandoned.

The depression stemmed in part from the harmful effects of the First World War on the British economy. Overseas markets had been lost and there was over-investment in the staple industries. The result was 'structural unemployment' (see page 50). Perhaps Britain needed new policies for a new age, and especially a regional policy to help the 'depressed areas'. But instead the Treasury tried to return to the past, to the policies pursued during the 'golden age' of the nineteenth century.

b) The Treasury View and Orthodox Economics

Treasury thinking derived from the so-called 'classical' school of economics which had grown up in the late eighteenth century. According to this viewpoint, the 'law' of supply and demand determined the workings of the economy: the demand for goods would always be roughly equal to the supply available, a balance that would be ensured by the price mechanism. Those with goods or services to sell would find a market at the 'best' price, that is, a price satisfactory to both buyer and seller. This was true whether an item for sale was a physical article or the labour of workers. Similarly, those who wanted to lend money and those who wanted to borrow would, in the end, agree on a rate of interest acceptable to each party. Interest rates (essentially the price at which money could be borrowed) would thus ensure that for every lender there would be a borrower. Indeed the whole economy would naturally be in a state of 'equilibrium'.

According to this theory, there might be economic crises, but the price mechanism of the market would ensure that they were short-lived. If, for instance, changes in the tastes of consumers meant that a certain article was no longer popular, then either the cost of the article would be lowered until it began to sell again or, eventually, the workers employed in manufacturing it would be thrown out of work. If the latter happened then, according to the classical economists, this should be readily accepted: there was no point in people working to produce what consumers did not want to buy. The result of redundancy would be a pool of cheap labour available to supply the real needs of the public. Thus unemployment would be merely temporary: it would cure itself because people out of work would be willing to work for lower-than-average wages and would thus soon find employment. If the whole of the economy went into recession, this too would, in the end, cure itself because of the price mechanism. In a slump prices would fall until people started consuming again, and in addition interest rates would fall until capitalists again found it profitable to borrow money and expand the economy.

Classical economists thus believed that the economy was self-correcting. Prosperity was natural, and slump and unemployment were unnatural and temporary aberrations. All was for the best in the best of all possible worlds – so long, that is, as governments followed a policy of *laissez-faire*, standing aside and allowing individuals to follow their own economic self-interest. If governments intervened too much, then the law of supply and demand would break down and the 'market economy' would cease to function.

The First World War had been a profound shock to orthodox economists. Victory in the war could not be left to natural market forces. The government could not stand aside and pursue a policy of *laissez-faire*: instead it had had to intervene and insist on the production of vital war materials, while at the same time increasing taxation and borrowing to pay for escalating expenditure (see page 35). It was all very distressing to the supporters of orthodox economics. Now, after the war and after the onset of the slump, they could return to 'sound finance'.

After the war civil servants at the Treasury had four main aims, which some have judged were held so tenaciously as to constitute dogma rather than reasoned judgements.

i) They wanted to see the budget balanced. The orthodox view was that no government should spend more than it raised in revenue through taxation. If a budget was unbalanced, government would have to borrow to pay for expenditure not covered by taxation, and this, it was thought, would have harmful consequences. The more demand there was to borrow, the higher interest rates would be – and high interest rates would deter businessmen from borrowing and investing for future growth. In addition, government loans would simply divert funds from other borrowers. Since governments would not use loans as constructively as private capitalists, an unbalanced budget would thus have harmful effects on the whole economy. Furthermore, most economists believed that 'expenditure' should include not merely spending on social services but the repayment of wartime debts or, at the very least, payment of interest on these debts. Otherwise the country would have to raise new loans to pay off old ones and would never be free of an escalating burden of debt.

ii) It was also thought desirable that a government should balance its budget at a low level of income and expenditure. The more government spent on services, the more it would have to tax the nation; and the more income taken by taxation, the less would be available for individuals to spend. If, because of heavy taxation, the demand for goods fell short of supply, then production would have to be cut back until equilibrium was reached once again. In short, government taxation interfered with the law of supply and demand. According to this view, governments could best help the economy by practising economy and refusing to spend above a bare minimum on administration, defence and social services.

iii) Another canon of economic orthodoxy was a belief in free trade: goods should be allowed freely to enter Britain from abroad, without the imposition of tariffs. It was thought that if Britain pursued free trade, then other countries would be more likely to follow this enlightened example, and the result would be the largest and most profitable market for British exports. In addition, it was believed that healthy competition from foreign imports would stimulate the modernisation of British industry.

iv) Finally, the Treasury was convinced that the value of the British currency, the pound sterling, should be maintained and that, if possible, there should be fixed exchange rates amongst the world's leading industrial nations, so as to facilitate international trade. These objectives, the civil servants believed, would lead to the return of business confidence and so to British prosperity. The means of achieving them was a return to the gold standard.

c) The Gold Standard

Civil servants believed that they should take a 'long view' of the economy: short-term political manoeuvres, while beloved of politicians especially at election time, were not in the real interests of the nation. They therefore wanted a policy which one official described as 'politician-proof' and which another more candidly called 'knave-proof'. The gold standard had provided such a policy. A country on the gold standard had to make three commitments: it would maintain its currency at the value of a fixed quantity of gold; it would allow the free convertibility of its currency into gold or into the currencies of other states on the gold standard; and finally it would link its money supply (the amount of notes in circulation) to the movement of gold in and out of the country. This system had provided for international financial stability in the nineteenth century and had minimised the degree to which governments interfered in the economy.

Like the classical economic model, the gold standard was self-regulating. Economic 'imbalance' would soon return to 'equilibrium'; or, put more simply, problems would sort themselves out. For instance, if a country on the gold standard had a sustained balance of trade deficit through importing more than it was exporting, then, under the rules of the system, gold would have to be exported to pay for the excess. This would automatically result in a reduction in the volume of currency in circulation, which in turn would produce a fall in the price of goods produced in Britain and thus lead to lower, more competitive export prices and to relatively higher, less competitive import prices. In consequence, the country would export more and import less – thus solving the original balance of payments problem. In addition, this mechanism was further bolstered by the idea that, if gold left the country, confidence in the pound would decline and the Bank of England (a private institution with the job of determining interest rates), having to retain the fixed value of the currency, would be forced to raise interest rates in order to discourage holders of sterling from switching their investments into other currencies ('a run on the pound'). These higher interest rates would then make credit more expensive and leave less money available for the purchase of goods, which would therefore tend to fall in price; and these lower prices would constitute another reason for overcoming the balance of payments crisis. The gold standard thus seemed the perfect mechanism for ensuring stability and prosperity.

d) The Return to Gold, 1925

The 'Treasury View' proved remarkably influential in the 1920s. Successive chancellors were careful to balance the budget and to avoid borrowing. It was said of Philip Snowden (the Labour Chancellor in 1924 and 1929–31) that he would 'no more have dreamt of budgeting for a deficit than of going into a public house'. The Conservative Chancellor from 1924 to 1929, Winston Churchill (who in fact drank a lot!) also believed that government expenditure was an evil, albeit a necessary one. Churchill's view was contained in the phrase 'Let the money fructify [be fruitful] in the pockets of the people'. Free trade was also accepted as orthodoxy for most of the decade. Industrialists who wanted protection against foreign imports were defeated.

The keystone of orthodox policy was the gold standard. During the war, when expenditure far exceeded gold reserves, the system could not operate effectively, and in 1919 Britain formally 'went off gold'. Since then problems for the British economy had multiplied. In particular, around one million men (ten per cent of the insured workforce) were regularly unemployed. The economy was refusing to obey the laws of classical economics. Unemployment should have corrected itself: the price mechanism should have led to more jobs, though at lower wages than before. What had gone wrong? Perhaps economic theory needed to be modified to take account of new realities. Yet most economists believed the main problem to be the absence of the gold standard. In the pre-war period, when this system had operated, Britain had been relatively stronger economically: sterling had been the most dominant international currency and the City of London had acted as banker to most of the world. Now the dollar and New York were more powerful. Hence in April 1925 the Treasury and the City persuaded Churchill to return Britain to the gold standard in the hope that pre-war prosperity would also return.

Equally significantly, they persuaded him to return at the 'pre-war parity'. This meant that the pound was valued at its pre-war level of 4.86 dollars. Churchill had been unsure about the return to gold at this now-fixed exchange rate. He once said that his advisers might just as well have been speaking in 'Persian' for all he understood of their complicated jargon. But in the end he consoled himself with the thought that the Governor of the Bank of England, Montagu Norman, and the leading Treasury official must know more about these complex matters than 'anyone else in the world'. Treasury experts were certain that, in the long run, the discipline imposed by the gold standard would benefit the British economy. Politicians would have less power to interfere, and manufacturers for export would have the benefits of a fixed exchange rate: their goods would cost a set amount abroad, instead of varying as the pound rose or fell in relation to other currencies. Yet few manufacturers had been consulted about the reform. Indeed, Norman went so far as to say that there was no need to seek manufacturers' opinions about the return to gold 'any more than about the design of battleships'! He was confident that he knew best. He and those who thought like him judged that the pound was being revalued in 1925: when sterling 'floated' in relation to other currencies it had had a lower exchange rate (varying from one foreign currency to another and being subject to fluctuations over time). It followed that henceforward British exports would cost more in overseas markets, but this did not seem a great problem. Other countries were expected to follow Britain's example and return to the gold standard at their pre-war parities and, moreover, higher export costs would do the British economy good.

The rationale for this view was that high wages were making the British economy sluggish and producing unemployment: they were responsible for blocking the natural tendency of the economy to return to equilibrium. Now, under the stimulus of a strong pound, employers would be forced to become more efficient and to cut wages. A general round of wage cuts, it was hoped, would reduce production costs and make British industry more competitive. Such cuts would lead to falls in the price of goods at home as well as abroad: in other words, wage reductions would not lead to cuts in the *standard* of living, for the *cost* of living would fall proportionately with wage reductions. The return to the gold standard would be an economic panacea. All would soon be well, or so it was hoped.

2 The Keynesian Alternative

a) Keynes and the Return to Gold

One economist – John Maynard Keynes – considered these Treasury arguments to be 'of the feather-brained order'. Indeed he thought that the return to the gold standard at the pre-war parity was a positive disaster. Keynes was the brilliant son of a wealthy Cambridge family, an aesthete and something of a philosopher as well as an economist. In 1919 he had attacked the Treaty of Versailles in *The Economic Consequences of the Peace*. Now, in 1925, he produced a pamphlet, *The Economic Consequences of Mr Churchill*. His argument was that, by returning to the gold standard at the pre-war parity, the pound was being over-valued by about ten per cent, necessitating a similar cut in wages which unions were bound to try to resist. The return to gold would thus produce intense industrial conflict, followed by wage cuts and unemployment. The mining industry, he predicted, would be the first to experience this strife.

1 Our export industries are suffering because they are the first to be asked to accept the 10 per cent reduction. If *every one* was

accepting a similar reduction at the same time, the cost of living
would fall, so that the lower money wage would represent nearly
5 the same real wage as before. But, in fact, there is no machinery
for effecting a simultaneous reduction. Deliberately to raise the
value of sterling money in England means, therefore, engaging in
a struggle with each separate group in turn, with no prospect that
the final result will be fair, and no guarantee that the stronger
10 groups will not gain at the expense of the weaker . . .
    On grounds of social justice, no case can be made out for
reducing the wages of the miners. They are the victims of the
economic Juggernaut. They represent in the flesh the 'fundamental adjustments' engineered by the Treasury and the Bank
15 of England to satisfy the impatience of the City fathers to bridge
the 'moderate gap' between $4.40 and $4.86 . . . The plight of the
coal miners is the first, but not – unless we are very lucky – the
last, of the Economic Consequences of Mr Churchill.
    The truth is that we stand mid-way between two theories of
20 economic society. The one theory maintains that wages should be
fixed by reference to what is 'fair' and 'reasonable' as between
classes. The other theory – the theory of the economic Juggernaut
– is that wages should be settled by economic pressure, otherwise
called 'hard facts', and that our vast machine should crash along,
25 with regard only to its equilibrium as a whole, and without
attention to the chance consequences of the journey to individual
groups.

    The attempt of the colliery owners to reduce wages in June 1925 –
and the subsequent General Strike – goes far to justify Keynes's
interpretation of the return to the gold standard. Most historians now
see the return to gold at the pre-war parity as an important cause of the
industrial strife of 1925–6 (see page 76). Even Churchill later admitted
that he had made the 'biggest blunder' of his life. Nevertheless the
significance of the return to gold has been disputed. One writer has
called the return 'the most dramatically disastrous error by a government in modern economic history', and another has called the miners a
'human sacrifice' to gold. But to some historians such judgements are
grossly exaggerated. They insist that Keynes miscalculated the over-
valuation of sterling, and that in reality it was revalued in April 1925 by
less than ten per cent. It is also possible that since British exports were
uncompetitive anyway, their new, higher price had little practical
effect. Some manufacturers may even have gained by having a fixed
exchange rate: at least the uncertainty associated with a floating pound
had disappeared, with a consequent boost to business confidence. Now
profits would depend on the volumes exported, not on the vagaries of
the exchange rate. And certainly import prices were lower, so home
consumers gained. One cautious historian has concluded that the return

to the gold standard was of no more than 'marginal significance in Britain's economic difficulties'.

Economic developments after April 1925 did not justify the return to gold. Other countries, including France and Belgium, followed Britain's example, but they returned at new parities. Certainly there was no return to Britain's nineteenth-century economic dominance, and nor could there have been since the basic causes of that dominance no longer existed. The Treasury had short-sightedly mistaken the symbol of British prosperity (the gold standard) for its root cause. As a result the British economy was handicapped: not only were exchange rates relatively high but interest rates had also to be kept high in order to protect the pound's fixed valuation. Under the gold standard regime, sterling could be freely converted into other currencies; and to prevent investors – some would say speculators – from switching from pounds to other currencies or to gold and producing a 'run on the pound', the Bank of England had to make it attractive for them to keep their investments in sterling by keeping interest rates – and thus the return on their investment – relatively high.

b) Keynesian Theory

Keynes was an unusual economist. Most academic economists were interested in theory, in economic models, and had a rather detached view of the real world. In general, they were wedded to the idea that economic problems would sort themselves out in the long run so long as governments practised *laissez-faire*. Keynes, on the other hand, had a highly developed social conscience: he believed that economics should serve social ends and should further human welfare. He therefore mocked the traditional view that, in time, the economy would always return to equilibrium. 'In the long run,' he retorted, 'we are all dead'. Keynes believed that progress and prosperity were far from inevitable. To his mind they were uncertain, just as the whole economic order was fragile. Observing in the mid-1920s that the economy seemed to have reached equilibrium at an unemployment level of one million workers, he could not believe that unemployment was unnatural or merely temporary. He therefore called for the end of *laissez-faire* and for governments to intervene energetically in order to minimise hardships and promote prosperity.

Keynes was in some ways an anti-theorist. In the 1920s he believed that all theories were inadequate because in the real world, as opposed to textbooks, there was always a large measure of uncertainty about economics. What was needed therefore was to face problems with the confidence that human ingenuity could find a solution. The German Chancellor Bismarck had once said that politics was 'the capacity of always choosing, in constantly changing situations, the least harmful, the most useful'. Keynes advocated such an approach for economics, and he was therefore a severe critic of the Treasury view.

By 1929 Keynes was convinced that governments should begin large-scale public works to provide jobs. To orthodox economists this proposition made no sense: it would involve borrowing money, and such money would merely be diverted from capitalist entrepreneurs to the government. Hence jobs created by public works would be matched by jobs lost as a direct result elsewhere in the economy. Keynes disagreed. He admitted that savings (that is, that proportion of people's income which was not spent on consumption) might be inelastic, but he argued that not all savings were currently being invested. Many people had money in current accounts – 'on deposit' – in the banks, rather than properly invested. There was therefore a surplus of savings which could be tapped for investment, and in his view government should do the tapping, borrowing the surplus savings and creating the jobs which so many people needed.

3 The Great Depression, 1929–32

a) The 1929 Election

Keynes not only opposed the Treasury view but also challenged politicians to act decisively to tackle the country's economic problems. The first to respond were Lloyd George and the Liberal Party. In the 1929 election Lloyd George stood on a manifesto called 'We Can Conquer Unemployment', aiming to reduce unemployment to 'normal proportions' within a year by an extensive scheme of public works. Keynes endorsed this programme. The other two parties, Labour and Conservative, stuck to traditional policies. Labour called for 'socialism', without having any real idea of how to achieve it. The Conservatives, the party in government, campaigned on the slogan 'safety first'. Churchill insisted that 'We should not try to compete with Lloyd George but take our stand on sound finance'. Conservatives took their lead from the Treasury, members of which defaced a copy of the Liberal manifesto with the words 'Extravagance, Inflation, Bankruptcy'. The Treasury continued to insist that governments could not safely create large numbers of extra jobs, as money to promote public works could either be borrowed, in which case it would be diverted from investment elsewhere and tend to push up interest rates, thus stifling economic growth; or it could be raised from taxation, and so reduce consumer spending and produce unemployment; or it could be printed, at the cost of inflation.

The Liberals improved their vote at the election but did not achieve power. Some believed that a golden opportunity had been lost to cure Britain's economic ills (see the cartoon on page 109). Labour won the largest number of seats, although without an overall majority, and

'*The lifeboat that stayed ashore*', *David Low cartoon, the* Evening Standard

formed the second Labour government. In effect the election saw a victory for 'economic conservatism' against 'economic radicalism', for both the Conservatives and Labour favoured traditional Treasury views. Keynes remarked that Snowden, the first supposedly socialist chancellor, was also the 'last adherent of true blue *laissez-faire*'.

b) Labour's Policies in the Depression

Labour had the difficult task of grappling with the Great Depression from October 1929. Unemployment mounted towards three million and foreign trade slumped alarmingly. J.H. Thomas, the new Minister for Employment, later wrote that 'I was facing a world economic blizzard that no man or government could cope with'. Many commentators also believed that there was no solution to these problems: after all, the depression was worldwide, and no country coped noticeably better than Britain in 1929–32.

Naturally the Treasury and the Bank of England believed that there was no political solution. They thought that the situation would eventually improve by itself and that meanwhile the government should observe the canons of sound finance, balancing the budget and encouraging workers to accept wage levels that would not result in their pricing themselves out of work. Above all, official advice was that the government should not indulge in financial gambles that would probably only make a bad situation worse. Such orthodoxy was certainly unimaginative, but even so it has been said that the Treasury (though not the Bank of England) was now becoming more flexible in its attitudes. Certainly its main objection to public works schemes was no longer based on economic principle but on administrative grounds. It was argued that public works on a large scale were simply impossible to organise in the short term, a view with which Herbert Morrison, Labour's Minister of Transport and an administrator of experience and skill, fully agreed. As a result, the government did not attempt to provide a large number of jobs by this method. Although expenditure on public works doubled from £70 million in February to £140 million in September 1930, this was insufficient even to prevent the unemployment totals from continuing to rise.

Another token effort was made at the end of 1929, when the Colonial Development Act made one million pounds a year available to promote development schemes in the British Empire. The aim was not so much to develop the colonies as to create jobs in Britain: it was hoped that the Act would create extra orders for British industry and so absorb unemployment. But the sums involved were so small, and grants to the colonies were hedged around with so many restrictions, that the effects of the scheme were negligible.

The Treasury's main advice was that the budget had to be balanced. This was very hard to achieve, for while government revenue from taxation was falling as more people became unemployed, the cost of unemployment benefit was escalating, from £12 million in 1928 to £125 million in 1931. Snowden wished to follow orthodox advice to scale down expenditure in general and the level of unemployment benefit in particular – in other words, to deflate the economy. But such cuts would be very unpopular with the bulk of the Labour Party, which regarded itself as the party of the underdog and the unemployed. The Chancellor therefore pursued a policy of 'drift'. No thorough or consistent policy was followed: instead the budget was left unbalanced for as long as possible.

Crisis came in 1931. A large deficit in the balance of payments was announced, while bank failures in Europe meant the loss of British investments. The pressure for Labour to balance its budget increased, especially when a royal commission on unemployment insurance called for reductions of up to 30 per cent in unemployment benefit. A month later, in July, the all-party May Commission painted a gloomy picture of the country's economic prospects, predicting a £120 million budget deficit for the coming year unless a 20 per cent cut was made in unemployment benefit.

Some traditional economists believed that unemployment benefit was preventing the economy from returning to equilibrium: men would not work for reduced wages when they had the 'dole' to fall back on. A cut might therefore put the economy back on its feet. Snowden, backed by Prime Minister Ramsay MacDonald, insisted that cuts in expenditure ('retrenchment') should replace drift. To make matters worse, a 'run on the pound' began: after the gloomy May Report foreign investors, fearing that Britain faced bankruptcy, began to withdraw funds in alarming quantities. By the end of July 1931 almost a quarter of the Bank of England's gold reserves had been used up. Snowden was convinced of the need to borrow money from international bankers to maintain the gold standard. He told the Cabinet that the loan was absolutely vital but that bankers in New York and Paris would only consent to lend the money if, first, expenditure was cut and the budget balanced.

Would a Labour Cabinet take the unpopular action of cutting unemployment benefit? In the summer of 1931 ministers were recalled from their holidays for key Cabinet meetings. But instead of decision there was deadlock. A group of ministers led by the Foreign Secretary, Arthur Henderson, would not accept cuts for the unemployed, and Ernest Bevin led a delegation from the Trades Union Congress (described by one irate minister as 'pigs') to lend its considerable weight to this resistance to cuts. The Cabinet split 12–9 in favour of a package of reductions totalling £78 million, including a ten per cent cut in unemployment benefit. Snowden later complained that a large number of his colleagues 'tamely submitted to the intimidation' of the TUC.

The TUC's position at their meeting with the Cabinet was voiced a fortnight later by its general secretary, Walter Citrine:

1 We were faced with the position either of accepting or rejecting the programme of cuts . . . Well, we wanted to assist the Government. None of us wanted to embarrass them more than they were obviously embarrassed at the moment But when you are faced
5 with a policy against which you have been fighting for years and which you know will be disastrous, no course is left open to you but unequivocally to say, as the General Council said, 'We cannot subscribe to this policy' . . . For years we have been operating on the principle that the policy which has been operated since 1925
10 in this country, of contraction, contraction, contraction, deflation, deflation, deflation, must lead us all, if carried to its logical conclusion, to economic disaster, and acceptance of this policy in

the judgement of the General Council would have tied us and anchored us to that principle, and logically we could not later
15 resist it when it spread to other channels.

The division in the Cabinet meant that MacDonald and Snowden were unable to secure acceptance for their proposals. Instead, on 24 August, they joined with Conservatives and Liberals in a coalition. The National Government was born.

c) The Alternatives to Orthodoxy, 1929–31

The Labour government had done little to tackle the Great Depression. They had avoided taking firm action, and when they could no longer drift along they had left office. It has been said that their socialism was impractical. Labour ministers could conjure up an appealing vision of a future socialist society of justice and harmony, and equally they could denounce the evils and inequalities of capitalism. But they could not offer coherent policies to bring about the transition from capitalism to socialism. However, the key question is whether the government could have done better. Were there other options open to them, besides the financial orthodoxy of the Treasury and the Bank of England?

The answer must be that there were. In 1930 the Prime Minister made former union leader J.H. Thomas head of a small ministerial team to tackle unemployment. The group included a wealthy 33-year old convert from the Conservative Party, Sir Oswald Mosley, and it was he who produced a memorandum of alternative proposals. Mosley wished to see protective tariffs to restrict imports, a greater use of credit to provide public works and promote expansion, more government direction of industry to promote rationalisation and efficiency, and increased pensions and allowances to boost domestic consumption and encourage earlier retirement. Borrowing ideas from Keynes, Lloyd George and the Conservative protectionists, he produced a positive package of proposals. However, his ideas were rejected by the Cabinet. Philip Snowden was firmly against such unorthodox ideas; the Prime Minister backed up the Chancellor; and Thomas – who got on very badly with his young assistant – also opposed the reforms. As a result, Mosley left the Labour Party and, despairing of democracy's capacity to achieve positive economic results, formed a fascist organisation (see *Britain: Domestic Politics, 1918–39* in this series for further details).

After the rejection of the Mosley Memorandum, MacDonald himself took responsibility for unemployment policy. The Prime Minister had never specialised in economic affairs and was in many ways out of his depth. He set up commissions and committees to investigate aspects of Britain's economic woes, but this was done merely to buy time. While the issues were being investigated, the government would survive – and possibly the depression might end by itself. Nevertheless MacDonald did receive advice which contrasted with Treasury thinking. There were two main sources for this. One was a 15-man Economic Advisory Council (a sort of economic 'think tank') and the other was the Committee on Finance and Industry, presided over by a judge, Lord Macmillan. Keynes was a prominent member of both of these bodies, and he was the main source of alternative economic ideas. An important confrontation took place when the Macmillan Committee questioned the Governor of the Bank of England. Montagu Norman made a bad showing: later he admitted that he had not even understood some of Keynes's questions. When asked on what theoretical basis he formed his judgements, the Governor simply tapped his nose and kept silent!

By now Keynes had strengthened his own theoretical ideas. In particular he began to develop what later became known as the 'multiplier effect', the idea that once people were set to work prosperity would be generated throughout the economy. New workers would also be consumers, and to supply their needs more men would be taken on who, in their turn, would become consumers, and so on – and on and on. Public works would have a valuable knock-on effect, but they could not be started unless the government agreed to finance them and so 'prime the pump'. Keynes was also becoming increasingly critical of the government's policy of high interest rates. These were needed to safeguard the gold standard, but at the same time they were stifling domestic investment. Even a member of the Bank of England admitted that high interest rates, while meeting their target, had unfortunate side-effects: they were 'a blunderbuss not a rifle'.

Keynes used two key words to summarise the differences between his views and those of the orthodox establishment – 'enterprise' and 'thrift'. The Treasury view was based on 'thrift', and this was a misguided policy because to cut benefits and wages in a depression would simply lower purchasing power and thereby reduce consumption and so throw more people out of work. For this reason he called the May Report 'the most foolish document I ever had the misfortune to read'. His own view was based on 'enterprise', and this led him to be attracted to a whole host of unorthodox proposals. In his own words, he 'twisted and turned to try to find some aid to the situation'. He favoured tariffs against foreign imports, so that domestic industry would be protected during the depression, and also recommended the use of large-scale public works. In fact, he told MacDonald that he was 'in favour of practically all the remedies which have been suggested'. He added that a negative attitude – 'the repelling of each of these remedies in turn' – was to his mind the only unforgivable sin.

In the crisis of August 1931, as the Cabinet was reaching deadlock over cuts in expenditure, Keynes recommended a further policy – that Britain abandon the gold standard. Snowden was insisting that Britain faced bankruptcy: there was a 'run on the pound' and Britain needed to borrow money from abroad, a precondition for which was a balanced budget. But, reasoned Keynes, this financial crisis was really artificial. If the pound were not tied to gold and to a fixed exchange rate, there would be no emergency. The pound would 'float' and find a realistic exchange rate, and furthermore Britain's domestic budget could be framed without regard to the wishes of overseas bankers. Moreover, Britain would then have control over its own interest rates, without the need to maintain the fixed exchange rate of sterling. In short, Keynes wished to see the sort of flexible response to the depression which the rigid gold standard system made impossible. But his advice was ignored.

Many figures on the left refused to countenance cuts in unemployment benefit from an instinctive, 'gut reaction' feeling that there had to be a better way to solve the country's problems than by inflicting hardship on people who were already the victims of capitalism. But not all who opposed the Treasury view did so for emotional reasons alone. Trade union leader Ernest Bevin had been a member of both the Economic Advisory Council and the Macmillan Committee, where he formed a close alliance with Keynes, and under his guidance TUC views were far more progressive than those of the Labour government. We can thus see quite clearly that alternative policies were open to MacDonald and his ministers. Yet they do not seem to have seriously considered them.

d) The Suspension of the Gold Standard

The National Government was formed on 24 August 1931 to take the action at which Labour had baulked. The new Cabinet, containing Labour, Conservative and Liberal ministers, was committed to economic orthodoxy. Philip Snowden, who continued as Chancellor, made economies of £70 million in government expenditure, including a ten per cent cut in unemployment benefit. He also increased taxation, lifting the standard rate of income tax from 22 to 25 per cent. These measures balanced the budget and allowed the government to negotiate a loan from abroad. Yet, to the surprise of ministers and the horror of Montagu Norman, Britain was soon forced off the gold standard.

Snowden's search for economies led him to cut the salaries and wages of government employees, and on 15 September British sailors in the fleet at Invergordon protested by refusing to obey orders. News of the 'Invergordon mutiny' produced a flight from sterling. This renewed 'run on the pound' depleted the country's gold reserves to such an extent that the Governor of the Bank of England decided that the gold standard would have to be suspended. Many people expected dire consequences to follow, including rapid inflation, and the pound fell from $4.86 to around $3.40. But it was soon realised that this 30 per cent devaluation was largely beneficial: it resulted in a more realistic exchange rate and it cushioned Britain from the effects of financial speculators. Several former Labour ministers were amazed at what had happened. 'Nobody told us we could do this', complained one. In fact Keynes had actually advised the Prime Minister to do precisely this.

Soon most people realised that the gold standard had been a 'sacred cow' which had needlessly complicated Britain's economic problems. It had been a mistake to return to gold at the pre-war parity in 1925 and foolish to retain the standard for so long. One element of dogma had been removed from financial thinking. Would the government henceforth play a more constructive role in the economy?

4 The Years of Recovery, 1932–9

What part did government play in Britain's recovery from the Great Depression? Did it remain true to the traditional Treasury view or did it show a willingness to adopt Keynesian techniques?

In fact Keynes's ideas were changing, and it was not easy to keep up with them. In 1936 his *General Theory of Employment, Interest and Money* was published. This was his most important publication – he believed it would over the next ten years 'largely revolutionise . . . the way the world thinks about economic problems' – but also one of his least accessible to the non-expert. Its basic idea was that the level of employment depended on the total of 'aggregate demand' in the economy – in other words, the total amount of spending (consumption and investment), whether by individuals or government. It followed from this that the government could, by spending enough, determine levels of employment, and this is exactly what Keynes urged should be done. Instead of simply balancing the budget by matching expenditure to income, government should manage the economy by influencing levels of aggregate demand. Put crudely, governments could generate full employment if they spent enough.

There were signs during the 1930s that politicians, taking their lead from Treasury officials, were becoming more open-minded. For instance, they were less opposed than hitherto to public works: indeed during the 1935 election campaign the Chancellor announced a five-year road-building programme costing £100 million. One expert, seeing the influence of Keynesian thinking in this scheme, has noted that 'the pillars of sound finance were no longer set in stone'. Nevertheless the pillars still existed. Many traditional views remained, alongside some new ideas. It is probably true to say that official economic policy was modified but not transformed.

a) The National Government's Economic Strategy

After the round of expenditure cuts and the ending of the gold standard in 1931, there were several noteworthy features to the government's economic strategy. The policy to which the government gave most prominence was unorthodox – a system of protection was introduced.

At the end of 1931 stop-gap measures were taken: the government was given the power to impose import duties at short notice on goods that were entering the country in 'abnormal' quantities. But early the following year the Import Duties Act imposed a general duty of ten per cent on all goods entering Britain, although goods from the British Empire were to be exempt, pending an imperial conference to be held in Ottawa later in the year. Many hoped that the Empire would become a self-supporting economic unit, enjoying free trade amongst its members while protected by tariff barriers against the rest of the world. But the conference proved disappointing. Dominions like Canada and Australia feared that if the Empire were free-trading, their own infant industries would suffer too much competition from British manufactured goods. As a result, they would not remove tariffs against British goods. Instead, they simply raised tariffs against non-British foreign items. Hence a measure of preference was given to imperial goods, but not an effective one. While it is true that during the rest of the 1930s Britain traded more than ever before with the Empire (so that exports to the Empire increased from 36 to 46 per cent of total trade between 1931 and 1938, and imports from the Empire over the same period rose from 25 to 38 per cent), the overall level of trade was not boosted. Most historians therefore agree that Britain's new tariff policy had little real effect on economic recovery.

More important were policies to which the government gave less attention. First, realising the benefits of a 'weaker' pound – in particular that exports were cheaper and therefore more competitive – the government took deliberate action through the Exchange Equalisation Fund to keep the value of the pound down, selling sterling when it looked likely to rise in value. This policy may have been of benefit to the economy, but its significance should not be exaggerated. After all, the recovery was essentially in industries producing for domestic consumption rather than for export (see page 66). Secondly, the government, no longer constrained by the gold standard, instituted a policy of low interest rates. Interest rates were lowered from six per cent in 1931 to two per cent the following year and were kept at this level until 1939.

Keynes approved both these aspects of government policy: they encouraged 'enterprise' rather than 'thrift'. But in fact the government also fostered an economic climate which discouraged borrowing and therefore probably hindered recovery. At the Exchequer Neville Chamberlain, Chancellor from 1931 to 1937, was a cautious man who, like his predecessors, believed in the importance of balanced budgets. He urged people to save and to 'tighten their belts' rather than spend. In his budget speech in 1932 he recommended 'hard work, strict economy, firm courage and unfailing patience' to the nation. The following year his message again comprised the same puritanical prescription. At the very time when Britain was emerging from the depression – because of the upturn in the trade cycle, the housing boom and the growth of expenditure on consumer goods (see pages 59–62) – the government was discouraging expansion. 'Aggregate demand' (to use Keynes's phrase) was growing, but it was fuelled by private rather than public spending.

b) The National Government's 'Unemployment Policy'

'Cyclical' unemployment disappeared as the 1930s wore on, but 'structural' unemployment remained at high levels (see page 55). The staple industries of coal, textiles, iron and steel, and shipbuilding remained depressed in the 1930s as they had been in the 1920s. The National Government made only a token effort directly to cure unemployment and to help the depressed areas. In 1934 the Special Areas Act made £2 million available in aid. As a result, about 44,000 workers were encouraged to move to other towns and another 30,000 were found places on retraining courses. Some improved social amenities, such as parks and swimming pools, were also provided. But the sums involved were small, areas like Lancashire (which Lancastrians judged to be a depressed area) were not included in the scope of the Act, and nothing substantial was achieved. The two unpaid commissioners who were responsible for implementing the legislation criticised its limitations and resigned in 1936. One of them insisted in his last report that 'We must not fear making a break with the traditions and practices of the past'.

Public criticisms led the government to pass the Special Areas (Amendment) Act in 1937. This tried to encourage firms to establish factories in the distressed areas by offering remission of rates, rent and income tax, up to 100 per cent for five years. But again little of substance was achieved. New trading estates were set up in South Wales, the North-East of England and in Scotland, but they employed hundreds rather than thousands. The Lord Mayor of Newcastle described it all as 'a mere flea-bite and a sop'. What really provided work in such areas was rearmament, and the unemployment problem was only really cured by the Second World War.

The Special Areas Acts produced cosmetic changes, and were designed to do no more. The government's low-key approach was a reflection of its general economic philosophy. It had decided not to attack the problem of unemployment directly. Its philosophy was summed up by Neville Chamberlain in 1935: 'The quickest and most effective contribution which any Government can make towards an increase of employment is to create conditions which will encourage and facilitate improvement in ordinary trade.' Despite tariffs and a managed exchange rate, the government remained true to the traditional notion that its essential task was to allow market mechanisms to function: in this way financial stability would encourage business confidence. It therefore had no 'employment policy' as such. Governments had a responsibility to relieve the poverty that stemmed from unemployment rather than to create jobs.

5 Conclusion: Governments and the Economy

Just as Britain's economic performance in the inter-war years has been the subject of contrasting verdicts, so has the role of governments in the economy. Governments have been praised for a good job well done and have also been condemned for woeful inadequacy. It is generally acknowledged that they made mistakes: the return to the gold standard at the pre-war parity was perhaps the most obvious. Furthermore, most experts on the inter-war years have concluded that politicians – including some chancellors – were out of their economic depth. They simply did not understand economic and financial mechanisms. But defenders insist that there were successes as well, and the inauguration of the Central Electricity Board in 1926 (see page 52) is widely regarded as one of the clearest examples.

Treasury policy did not remain static during this period. Official thinking developed and became more flexible (especially as the 1930s wore on), and more willing to plan for economic growth. Indeed 'planning' is often said to be one of the keynotes of political economy in the 1930s.

The key issue is whether – especially during the Great Depression – governments ignored viable solutions to Britain's problems. Would a more positive, Keynesian thrust have produced greater economic success? In particular, would mass unemployment have been cured or at least alleviated? If so, then governments should rightly be condemned for tolerating such high levels of unemployment and for accepting levels of economic growth far below the optimum of which the British economy was capable.

a) Did Keynes Have the Answers?

The response to this question has varied over several decades. Until the early 1970s, it was believed by most historians that Keynes had undoubtedly been right. Keynes became an economic adviser to the Treasury in 1940, and his thinking then dominated economic strategy. Britain experienced high levels of employment from 1940 until the late 1960s: this was the 'age of Keynes', and it was assumed that never again would Britain have to tolerate mass unemployment. During this period the record of the inter-war years, and particularly the 1930s, seemed especially poor. Governments had ignored the realistic policies which Keynes had presented to them. Hence politicians were the 'guilty men' who had sacrificed a generation of working people on the altar of

Treasury dogma. No criticism seemed too harsh for them, and no praise too great for Maynard Keynes.

However, during the 1970s economists became divided, and many if not most began to see fatal flaws in Keynes's theories. The world was now in the 'post-Keynesian age'. In particular it was said that Keynes's ideas produced inflation. His emphasis on 'demand' produced not greater 'supply' but price rises – and such inflation could only be cured by higher interest rates and, ultimately, by the very unemployment his policies were designed to eliminate. As Keynes had previously been excessively praised, so now he was excessively condemned as an essentially arrogant man whose social concerns had led him to misjudge what was feasible in the real world. Many economists decided that the orthodox views of the inter-war period had been correct: governments should stand aside and let businessmen produce jobs and prosperity. Several historians have now reinterpreted 1918–39 to show that the Treasury, while making some mistakes, had been broadly correct to insist on balanced budgets and 'sound finance' – and to be wary of Keynes's 'solutions'.

The issue is confusing to non-experts. Perhaps the most acceptable view lies somewhere between the extremes. Keynes had exposed the rigidities in Treasury thinking between the wars, especially the naive view that the economy would return to 'equilibrium' at full employment if left alone. It made little sense to continue to look upon unemployment as a temporary aberration that would cure itself when over a million men were continuously out of work for well over a decade. On the other hand, Keynes did not have all the answers, and he probably failed to take sufficient account of business confidence. Indeed it may well be true, as one historian has argued, that had Keynes's views been applied in the circumstances of July 1931 their sheer novelty and the abhorrence with which most bankers and businessmen viewed them might well have led to economic collapse. Furthermore, while the stimulation of 'aggregate demand' might well have led to economic expansion, there was no guarantee that this would not have produced even greater growth in the South East while leaving the depressed areas still depressed. Keynes's other main idea – government-sponsored public works – would not have revived the ailing staple industries and might well have created administrative difficulties that would have diminished their impact. In short, Keynesian thinking was much more relevant to 'cyclical' than to 'structural' unemployment.

b) Assessment

Governments between the wars, with the exception of the Lloyd George coalition in 1918–20, followed cautious policies. 'Safety first' was their watchword. Probably they were over-cautious: on the whole, they were unwilling to experiment. Though there is room for argument, it is probably true to say that the policies pursued by governments to combat depression neither helped nor hindered the economy to any great extent. The politicians may have settled for this verdict. On the whole they were fearful men, and it must be admitted that there was much to be fearful of. There was runaway hyperinflation in Germany in the early 1920s; the collapse of banks in 1929–32; and mass discontent leading to political upheaval and even revolution in several European countries. In Britain, traditional policies sacrificed the possibility of economic revival to minimise the possibility of economic collapse. Perhaps politicians were wrong to be so cautious, but it is hard to blame them for not throwing in their lot with untried and untested policies. They received an enormous amount of advice and, while it was conflicting, most of it was in favour of orthodoxy. Keynes was not quite a 'voice in the wilderness', especially from 1932 onwards, but he was always in a minority.

Keynes had made a fortune on the stock market by 1936, but he had earlier lost a fortune in 1921. Had he converted governments to his ideas, Britain might have undergone economic revival and transformation between the wars. The 'Hungry Thirties' might never have existed. On the other hand, there might have been collapse and disaster: the very real improvements in British industry and in the standard of living experienced by most peoples in the 1930s might never have materialised. No one can really be sure what the results would have been had different polices been pursued, although it is fascinating for historians and economists to speculate. However, politicians felt they had to be circumspect in dealing with national finances.

Making notes on 'Governments and the Economy'

The headings and sub-headings given in the chapter should help you to organise your notes. Pay particular attention to (i) the return to the gold standard in 1925 and (ii) the depression of 1929–32. In your concluding section, you should reach *your* own conclusion: do not be afraid to disagree with the cautious views the author has presented.

This chapter deals not just with events but also with economic theory. The important thing is to grasp the essential mechanisms involved in both the orthodox Treasury view and in the Keynesian alternatives. You might experiment with different ways of noting the main principles in each. Might a diagram help more than straightforward prose? You should also ensure you understand the simple economic processes involved in both schools of thought. Do you understand, for instance, the major economic effects of variations in the

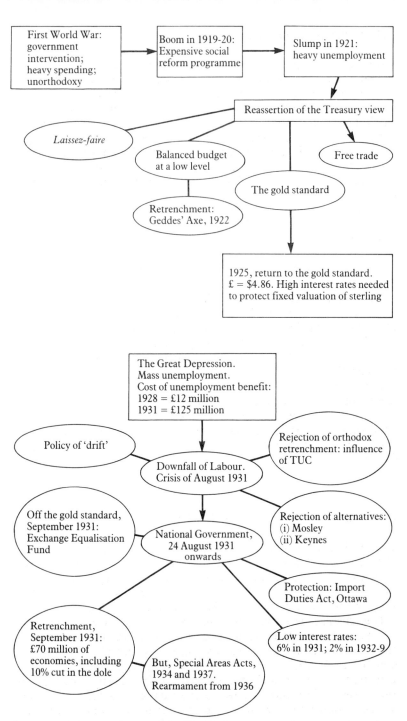

First World War: government intervention; heavy spending; unorthodoxy → Boom in 1919-20: Expensive social reform programme → Slump in 1921: heavy unemployment

Reassertion of the Treasury view

Laissez-faire

Balanced budget at a low level

Free trade

The gold standard

Retrenchment: Geddes' Axe, 1922

1925, return to the gold standard. £ = \$4.86. High interest rates needed to protect fixed valuation of sterling

The Great Depression. Mass unemployment. Cost of unemployment benefit:
1928 = £12 million
1931 = £125 million

Policy of 'drift'

Downfall of Labour. Crisis of August 1931

Rejection of orthodox retrenchment: influence of TUC

Off the gold standard, September 1931: Exchange Equalisation Fund

National Government, 24 August 1931 onwards

Rejection of alternatives:
(i) Mosley
(ii) Keynes

Protection: Import Duties Act, Ottawa

Retrenchment, September 1931: £70 million of economies, including 10% cut in the dole

But, Special Areas Acts, 1934 and 1937. Rearmament from 1936

Low interest rates: 6% in 1931; 2% in 1932-9

Summary – Governments and the Economy

level of interest rates – on price and employment levels? If you are confident of the theory, your notes can be much briefer than if you are less sure.

You might add several technical terms to your personal glossary. To get full benefit from this chapter, it should be read in conjunction with Chapter 4. You might also wish to obtain further details on political issues by consulting the companion volume *Britain: Domestic Politics, 1918–39*.

Answering essay questions on 'Governments and the Economy'

This is a popular topic with examiners. Sometimes questions can encompass the whole of the inter-war period. Consider the following titles:

1 Explain why politicians failed to solve the problem of unemployment between the wars.
2 With what success did successive governments tackle Britain's economic problems between the two World Wars?

While covering the same chronological period, these titles require very different emphasis. Try to write a brief concluding paragraph for each of them, bringing out as clearly as you can the differences of approach that each necessitates. Remember that these questions relate not just to government policy but to British economic performance: you will need to be familiar with Chapter 4 as well as this one.

Other titles are narrower and more specific:

3 To what extent was the return to the gold standard in 1925 a major cause of the depression of the 1930s?
4 Did the national governments of the 1930s deal with economic problems more effectively than their Labour predecessors?
5 'Economic recovery in the 1930s owed little to the actions of governments.' Discuss.
6 How well did the National Government deal with the economic crisis of 1931?

Consider each of these titles in turn. Try a 'brain-storming' session to pinpoint the various arguments you could put forward, and then go on to establish which ones you could argue effectively. Then, when you have sorted out your views, try to work out a paragraph-by-paragraph plan for each title. Arguments and plans for questions 3 and 5 should pose few problems: as well as examining the precise issues to which you are directed, you have to examine alternative explanations and causes as well. Nevertheless, even if you think the return to the gold standard and the actions of governments were unimportant, you must spend a reasonable portion of the essay discussing these issues. The questions necessitate this. Question 4 is more tricky. You will probably have paragraphs on the actions of the two Labour governments, as well as the national governments; but will you have paragraphs on the nature and severity of economic problems in particular periods? Will you include a section on the way in which the advice of the 'experts' changed? Question 6 is also challenging, and you will have to resist the temptation to extend the title from 1931 to cover a wider area. Nevertheless, by examining the nature of the 1931 crisis you can make your knowledge of the earlier and later periods relevant. Did the National Government handle the crisis of 1931 in such a way as to ensure that there were longer-term economic benefits, or was it simply concerned with immediate survival? Can you make a consideration of Keynes's ideas relevant? Could you even make Keynes central to your answer?

Source-based questions on 'Governments and the Economy'

1 Keynes on the return to gold
Read the extracts from *The Economic Consequences of Mr Churchill* given on page 106. Answer the following questions:
a) Explain why workers in the 'export industries' (line 1) would be asked to accept wage cuts before workers in other industries. (*2 marks*)
b) What do you think Keynes meant by the 'economic Juggernaut' (lines 13 and 22)? (*2 marks*)
c) Do you find Keynes's arguments in the extract to be persuasive? Explain your answer. (*6 marks*)

2 Low on Treasury Dogma
Study the cartoon, *The Lifeboat That Stayed Ashore* by David Low, reproduced on page 109. Answer the following questions:
a) Explain what you consider the overall message of the cartoon to be. (*4 marks*)
b) How far do the words held up by Winston Churchill sum up Treasury policy in 1929? (*2 marks*)
c) Comment on the depiction of Churchill's crew of the lifeboat. What point was Low attempting to make by drawing them as he did? (*4 marks*)
d) In what ways does the depiction of Keynes and Lloyd George (the other sailor) accurately reflect their aims and actions in 1929? (*5 marks*)

3 Citrine on the TUC during the 1931 crisis

Read the extract from Citrine's speech in early September 1931, on pages 111–12. Answer the following questions:

a) Was Citrine correct to describe government policy after 1925 as contraction and deflation (line 10)? Explain your answer. *(3 marks)*

b) Explain why Citrine thought that expenditure cuts would lead to 'economic disaster' (line 12). *(3 marks)*

c) Comment on the 'tone' of the speech. In particular, assess the extent of Citrine's hostility towards the Labour government. *(4 marks)*

CHAPTER 7

Conclusion

Historians spend much of their time pursuing detailed studies, sometimes 'examining the frontiers of knowledge with a microscope'. Such
activity is vital, for without original research history would become
merely a re-telling of familiar tales with no infusion of new evidence.
Nevertheless it is also necessary for historians to raise their eyes from
matters of detail in order to consider broader issues. Too exclusive a
concern with specialised matters is liable to make historical study, in
the words of one critic, 'a pedantic search after the insignificant'. There
are therefore times when we should substitute the telescope for the
microscope. In this book we have examined Britain's economic performance and industrial relations over four decades. What conclusions
can be reached about the period as a whole?

Several themes should be singled out. On the economic side, there is
the issue of Britain's decline from its nineteenth-century pre-eminence.
From about 1880 Britain had begun to lose its economic lead over
potential rivals. What role did 1900–39 play in this 'relative decline'?
More generally, how successful was the British economy during these
years, and how did economic performance affect the standard of living
in Britain? Another key issue is the role of governments in the
economy. How important was 1900–39 in the growth of government
interventionism, and how successful were politicians in this (by
nineteenth-century standards) unaccustomed role?

In the field of industrial relations several issues must be addressed.
The position of trade unions in law was ambiguous in 1900 – what
clarification had been made by 1939? How had the role of the unions
changed by this date? We must also consider, more generally, the
changing state of industrial relations in the period 1900–39 and in
particular the degree of co-operation and of conflict that existed
between employers and workers.

1 The Economy

a) Relative Decline

During the last quarter of the nineteenth century Britain lost the
enormous economic lead which it had enjoyed over all other countries.
By 1914 the USA and Germany (in some industries) had overtaken its
manufacturing output. Yet, on the eve of war, Britain still enjoyed a
lead over its competitors in certain spheres (such as finance), and per
capita it was still a more highly industrialised country than all others
apart from the United States. However, by 1939 it had fallen further
behind the USA, it had a smaller share of world manufacturing output

than Germany, and it had also been overtaken as an economic power by the Soviet Union.

What had gone wrong? Many answers have been given by historians. Perhaps the most persuasive of these is that British industry failed to modernise. In particular the old staple industries, which had spearheaded the country's economic success in the Victorian era, became technologically backward and lost export markets overseas. In many ways businessmen were short-sighted. The staple industries enjoyed a boom immediately after the First World War, and many industrialists believed that the best days were still ahead for British coal, iron and steel, textiles, and shipbuilding. It took a long time for them to be convinced otherwise.

Britain's relative decline is a fascinating theme, but it has probably attracted too much of the attention of historians studying the years 1900 to 1939. There were also successes in this period, including the growth of new consumer goods industries and improved productivity in many industries, and these should not be ignored. Britain's share of world manufacturing output fell over the period as a whole, but it increased between 1928 and 1938, and by this latter date the country was no longer declining *vis-à-vis* its rivals. The fact that larger states with more abundant raw materials were producing more than Britain was hardly an indictment of the British economy: instead, it was perfectly natural. Only the USSR had overtaken Britain's industrial production between the wars, and then only at the tremendous human cost involved in Stalin's five-year plans. Living standards were certainly far higher in Britain than in Soviet Russia. British growth rates may seem unspectacular when compared with those achieved in Stalin's Russia or Hitler's Germany, but then Britain was a democracy while they were dictatorships, and the price to be paid for democracy – which allows individuals to make free economic as well as political choices – is often some degree of economic confusion.

Some measure of relative decline was inevitable after the enormous but 'unnatural' lead established in the middle of the previous century. 1880–99 saw this trend established. 1900–39 saw a further relative decline – although the economy continued to grow – but it was hardly a catastrophic one. There was greater relative decline in the 1920s than in the 1930s: in short, the decline was slowing down by 1939, not speeding up. Only in the 1950s and 1960s – when, paradoxically, affluence for the bulk of the British public reached hitherto unprecedented levels – did relative decline accelerate alarmingly, and the reasons for this must be sought in the period after 1940 not before.

b) Unemployment and Poverty

Undoubtedly there was economic success as well as failure between 1900 and 1939, and even during a period of relative decline there were increases in the standard of living. The real shortcoming was Britain's poor record in the realm of unemployment. Cyclical levels were bad, with peaks in 1921 and 1930–2, but structural unemployment resulted in over one million people being continuously out of work. Poverty had been most commonly caused by low wages before 1914; after 1918 unemployment was its major cause. As a result, there existed in one of the richest countries in the world what one historian has called 'a submerged, slum-dwelling, under privileged, ignorant and under-nourished minority'. In this period between 15 and 30 per cent of the population lived in poverty or near to it.

A defence can be made of the period after the First World War. Statistics make the problem seem relatively worse than it was. The available figures suggest that in the best years of the inter-war period unemployment rates were higher than in the worst years of the late nineteenth and early twentieth centuries. However, before 1921 we only have totals of trade union members out of work, whereas from 1921 onwards we have the much more representative totals of insured workers who were unemployed. Almost certainly, therefore, more workers were unemployed before 1921 than we are aware of. The number out of work should also be assessed in the light of the changing age-structure of Britain's population. While in 1911 64 per cent of the population were aged 15–64, this figure had risen to 70 per cent by 1939. The potential labour force over this period grew by about two million. Yet by the end of the 1930s more people than ever before in Britain's history had found work. Furthermore, the new jobs that were being created tended to be in the highly productive and capital-intensive 'new industries', so that in fact the very success of British industry – in becoming mechanised rather than relying on large numbers of workers – was tending to limit employment opportunities. It should also be said, in defence of the period, than a man on the dole in 1939 was better off, in real terms, that a fully employed labourer in 1900. Nevertheless, even when all these factors are taken into account, it must be admitted that Britain's employment record was poor. Mass unemployment existed not only during recessions and depressions, when almost every country suffered from similarly high totals, but during periods of economic buoyancy, when Britain's rivals approached full employment. It took the Second World War to bring new economic life to the 'depressed areas'.

In many ways the economic picture of 1900–39 is a black and white one of sharply contrasting features: affluence and poverty, boom and bust, growth and decay. Yet all too often polemical writers have portrayed it in terms of black *or* white.

c) Government Involvement

Government economic policies varied greatly during the period from

1900 to 1939. *Laissez-faire* gave way to full-scale mobilisation of the country's economic resources during the First World War, and in 1918–20 it seemed that the government would continue an active, interventionist role. 1921, when boom gave way to bust, was therefore a turning point of major significance, allowing traditional ideas to reassert themselves. Politicians attempted to 'return to normalcy' – when arguably they should have been forging new policies relevant to Britain's new economic position – culminating in the return to the gold standard in 1925. Yet government activity could not return to pre-war levels, partly due to the fact that in an age of universal suffrage politicians had to be responsive to the wishes of the electorate. (Cynics – or perhaps realists – would say that they had to 'buy votes' to stay in power.) The standard rate of income tax, which had been six per cent in 1910–14, averaged about 25 per cent in 1918–39, making revenue available for new social services.

Throughout the inter-war period a debate took place on the degree to which governments should seek to influence economic trends. Keynes was the foremost proponent of active intervention: casting scorn on unimaginative Treasury 'thrift', he believed that unemployment could be significantly reduced by public works and other methods. Government ministers and Treasury officials were influenced but not converted by his thinking. Perhaps a golden opportunity was missed. Politicians before 1939 tended to favour traditional, conservative economic policies. They quite openly preferred to tolerate high levels of unemployment in order to minimise the risks of financial and economic collapse. They simply hoped that one day market forces would provide extra employment opportunities. 'There is little governments can do . . .' insisted the fatalistic Stanley Baldwin. In fact he and other politicians were forgetting the lessons of 1914–18, when governments had done a great deal. During the Second World War, the Treasury turned to radical, Keynesian economic policies, and in 1944, the government felt confident enough of its powers to promise to maintain a 'high and stable level' of employment after the war. If only such confidence had existed earlier, perhaps the mass unemployment of the 1920s and 1930s could have been avoided. State-sponsored modernisation of the economy (as favoured by Keynes, Lloyd George and Oswald Mosley) might have produced far greater economic progress than was in fact achieved.

In defence of governments, it should said that the Second World War, like the First, created a wholly new psychological climate. In 1940 Britain was fighting for its life, and it was the new political agenda ('victory at all costs . . . for without victory there is no survival') which prescribed new economic strategies. It must also be recognised that the promise in 1944 to maintain full employment, though successful for 20 years, now looks like a sick joke. We all know much more about economics and finance than was known in 1900–39 (or at least we think we do), but those who make bold assertions about past mistakes are apt to be discomfited when unexpected twists in present-day economic fortunes shed new light on past issues. Fools are likely to rush in where cautious historians fear to tread! Above all, we must always remember that the people making the decisions at the time did not have the benefit of the historian's hindsight. Developments which are now in the past for us were for them in the future – and this makes a big difference. This is not to say that viable opportunities were not missed in 1900–39 or that politicians should not be criticised: it is simply to urge that we should make an attempt to see issues with the perspectives of the policy-makers themselves.

Another possible missed opportunity was Britain's failure to develop the potentially rich resources of its empire. Politicians in Whitehall had little control over the self-governing Dominions (like Canada and Australia). But there were many dependent colonies whose economies Britain could control. In the 1890s Joseph Chamberlain had referred to 'our undeveloped estate', and by 1939 very little had been done to produce economic growth. The ideal colony, from Whitehall's point of view, was simply one that balanced its budget and so did not require grants-in-aid from Britain. Whether it was rich or poor, developing or stagnant, was of entirely secondary consideration. 'Our crime isn't exploitation,' said Ernest Bevin about the colonial empire; 'It's neglect.' There were climatic and other constraints against economic development, and indeed when in 1947–51 Bevin and other Labour ministers attempted to grow groundnuts on a large scale in Africa, their efforts proved to be an expensive failure. But since no real attempts were made in 1900–39 to foster the economic development of the colonies – certainly not by the Colonial Development Act of 1929, with its miserly funding level of one million pounds a year – it is impossible to prove whether or not an important opportunity was missed.

2 Industrial Relations

a) Legislation

Between 1900 and 1939 the legal position of trade unions was greatly clarified. By 1913 it was accepted that unions could use 'peaceful picketing' during strikes (though what this meant in practice was still open to some dispute); they could not be prosecuted for losses incurred by employers during strikes; and they could impose the 'political levy'. However, the rules governing payment of the levy were changed by the Trade Disputes Act of 1927. Henceforth 'contracting in' for those who wanted to pay replaced 'contracting out' for those who did not. This Act was a victory for right-wingers in Britain, but in contrast with developments in Nazi Germany and elsewhere in fascist Europe – where strikes were banned and free trade unions forbidden – it was a small enough defeat for the unions. The 1927 law also ensured that there would be further legislation: the Labour Party promised to repeal the Act when next it formed a majority government. It did so in 1946.

b) The Growth of Trade Unions

Membership of trade unions fluctuated broadly in line with levels of employment and economic prosperity. Membership peaked in 1921, at 8,350,000, just as the economic boom was coming to an end. It did not reach that level again until 1947. Defeat in the General Strike in 1926 lowered the prestige of trade unionism, while the depression of 1929–32 further weakened the movement. Membership sank to 4,400,000 in 1934. But then there was a recovery, so that by 1939 there were more than three times as many union members as in 1900. By the end of our period, therefore, trade unions had become an accepted feature of Britain's economic landscape, recognised by the great majority of the country's employers, who negotiated with them to determine rates of pay. Although many people tend to remember the spectacular union defeats of 1900–39, the truth of the matter is that only the most optimistic union leaders of 1900 could have hoped to achieve the level of support and authority that the trade union movement had established by 1939.

1914–18 saw the unions at the peak of their influence with government, but they were politically influential at other times too, especially in 1931 and again in 1936–9. Having founded the Labour Representation Committee in 1900 – so that, in Bevin's words, the Labour Party 'sprang from the bowels' of the trade union movement – the unions were from 1935 taking a key role in guiding the Party. During the Second World War the unions were to be more influential with government than ever before. In 1940 Bevin became Minister of Labour and began a ten-year alliance with the Labour leader Clement Attlee, which turned out to be undoubtedly the most constructive political partnership in modern British history.

c) Victory for the Moderates

1900–39 saw a victory for 'moderate' trade unionism. Syndicalists and other radicals, seeking to overthrow capitalism and establish workers' control of industry, had been defeated. They had come nearest to success when strikes gripped industry in 1911–12 and 1920–21. For a time during the First World War it seemed that they might exert greater influence on rank and file members than the official union leaders, and they might have become more influential had the General Strike lasted longer. But probably their influence has been exaggerated by left-wing writers sympathetic to their cause, and certainly by 1935 the moderate, 'collaborationist' leaders like Bevin and Citrine effectively dominated the trade union movement. By then trade unions were reformist rather than revolutionary: indeed, instead of providing an alternative to the capitalist economy, they had become an important element in capitalism. Marx had predicted that greedy capitalists would exploit their workers more and more until they rose up in a bloody revolution, but effective trade unionism (among other factors) ensured that workers had far more to lose than simply their chains.

The syndicalists may well have prevented the achievement of greater harmony in industrial relations, for notions of worker control and even worker participation in management decisions were damned by association with them. Instead the unions remained sharply divided from management, perpetuating the 'us' and 'them' attitude which has bedevilled industrial relations in Britain. Opportunities were missed before 1939 to break down this divide. The 'triangular collaboration' of 1914–18 (between government, businessmen and unions) led nowhere, the joint industrial councils of the same period soon ceased to function, and the Mond–Turner talks had few positive consequences. These were significant failures. The nationalised sectors of the economy (like the Central Electricity Board and the British Broadcasting Corporation) were run by boards of directors, just like private companies. After the Second World War, when Attlee's Labour governments of 1945–51 nationalised about 20 per cent of industry (including the coal industry, thus belatedly fulfilling the recommendations of the 1919 Sankey Commission), the same form of nationalisation was favoured, without any form of worker participation in management. The precedents of the inter-war years had been followed. Arguably an important opportunity had been missed to generate better industrial relations by destroying the sharp division between 'employers' and 'employees'.

British industry was, in varying degrees, strike-prone in 1900–39. The stoppages of these years contributed to Britain's relatively poor economic performance. Certainly the loss of 162 million working days during 1926, the year of the General Strike, must have prevented the full force of the worldwide upturn in the trade cycle affecting Britain. Nevertheless, unions and employers managed in the end to establish some sort of *modus vivendi*. This system of industrial relations was in many ways muddled, inefficient and unsatisfactory. Class antagonism was a potent force between the wars, though 'class war' (a term employed by many historians of the period) seems to be an exaggeration, certainly after 1926. Nevertheless, there was a positive side to this picture as well. The right to withdraw one's labour was an action which some felt was being exercised all too often in Britain, but it was also a precious freedom all too rare in Europe in the 1920s and especially in the 1930s. Strikes were a sign that the British enjoyed a political freedom that was signally lacking in several other European countries.

From 1940 to 1945 Britain's economy and industrial relations system were to be challenged as never before in their history, and by a supposedly ultra-efficient totalitarian regime, in which the government controlled the economy and industrial relations. The fact that Britain was able to mobilise a higher percentage of its economic resources for war than Nazi Germany and at key times to 'out-produce' its enemy, and to do so by more democratic and voluntary means, does not reflect badly on the 1900–39 period.

Working on 'Conclusion'

You will not need to make detailed notes on this chapter, since it only provides a small amount of new factual information. Instead, you need to engage yourself with the basic issues: (i) the role of 1900–39 in Britain's relative decline, (ii) Britain's overall economic performance and the significance of mass unemployment, (iii) the changing role of governments, and (iv) the changing pattern of industrial relations. On all of these issues, you need to formulate your own judgements on the basis of the evidence at your disposal rather than tamely accept what other people think.

Two issues are worth thinking about. First, the importance of assessing not only what happened but, occasionally, what did not. Do you agree that in 1900–39 there were important missed opportunities? By highlighting these, we can sometimes appreciate much more fully the significance of what did occur. Secondly, the need for comparisons in forming opinions should be considered. In this chapter (though all too briefly) the British experience in 1900–39 is compared with that before and after these years and also with what was happening elsewhere at the same time. Do you see the need for this? Can you think of other comparisons? The problem with this method, of course, is that it requires knowledge of these other areas – but then the quest for historical understanding is a never-ending one!

Chronological Table

1900   Labour Representation Committee set up.
Two million trade union members.

1902   Taff Vale case: unions liable for damages.

1906   Trade Disputes Act, reversing Taff Vale.

1909   Osborne Judgement, against financial support from the unions to the Labour Party.

1910   Miners' strikes: one man killed at Tonypandy, two at Llanelli.

1911   Eleven million days lost in strikes.
Dockers' strike: three killed.
National rail strike.
Payment for MPs.

1912   41 million days lost in strikes.
National miners' strike, followed by Coal Mines Act.

1913   Trade Union Act, reversing the Osborne Judgement: trade unions could impose a 'political levy'.
Transport strike in Dublin: two killed.

1914   Four million trade union members.
April, 'triple alliance' formed: miners, railwaymen and transport workers.
August, outbreak of the First World War.

1915   Strikes on the Clyde.
March, 'Treasury Agreement'.
May, Lloyd George became Minister of Munitions.
July, Munitions of War Act, banning strikes and making dilution compulsory.

1916   December, Lloyd George became Prime Minister.

1917   May, engineering strikes in Coventry, Manchester and Sheffield.

1918   Six million trade union members.
11 November, end of First World War.

1919   Restoration of Pre-War Practices Act.
January, strike for 40-hour week in Glasgow.
31 January, 'Bloody Friday' – riot in George Square, Glasgow.
February, miners' threat of a strike with support of triple alliance: government set up the Sankey Commission.

1920   Economic boom.
Formation of the Communist Party of Great Britain.
General Council of the TUC set up.
May, dockers refused to load the *Jolly George*, as part of the 'Hands Off Russia' campaign.

1921   Eight million trade union members.
85 million working days lost in strikes.
1 April, the day of 'decontrol' of the mines: national miners' strike began.
15 April, 'Black Friday': triple alliance collapsed.
June, two million unemployed.
1 July, defeated miners returned to work.

1922   Transport and General Workers' Union formed, led by Bevin.
February, the 'Geddes' Axe'.

1924   The Dawes Plan, leading to the export of free German coal.

1925   Only eight million working days lost in strikes.
April, return to the gold standard (£ = $4.86). Keynes responded with *The Economic Consequences of Mr Churchill*.
June, colliery owners called for lower wages. Government responded with the Macmillan inquiry.
31 July, 'Red Friday': Baldwin granted subsidy of £23 million to the mining industry. Samuel Commission set up.

1926   Creation of the Central Electricity Board.
11 March, Samuel Report published.
30 April, colliery owners began a lock-out; government declared a state of emergency; TUC promised to support the miners.
3 May, unofficial strike at the *Daily Mail*: government ended negotiations with the TUC.
4 May, General Strike began.
5 May, Sir John Simon insisted a general strike was illegal.
12 May, TUC called off the General Strike.
13 May, a second, and spontaneous, strike.
December, last miners returned to work, accepting lower wages, longer hours and district agreements.

1927   Trade Disputes Act.

1929   Colonial Development Act.
30 May, general election: the second (minority) Labour government.
24 October, 'Black Thursday': US stock market collapsed.

1931   Three million unemployed (22% of insured workforce).
July, May Report (calling for a 20% cut in the dole), leading to a 'run on the pound'.
23 August, Labour Cabinet split 12–9 over expenditure cuts totalling £78 million (including 10% cut in dole).
24 August, MacDonald formed National Government.
15 September, the 'Invergordon Mutiny'.
21 September, Britain went off the gold standard.

1932   Import Duties Act (10% tariff on most non-empire imports).
August, Ottawa economic conference.

1934   4,400,000 trade union members (lowest point between the wars).
       Less than one million working days lost in strikes (fewer than in any previous year this century).
       Special Areas Act: £2 million available in aid to some of the depressed areas.
1936   Keynes, *General Theory of Employment, Interest and Money*.
1937   Special Areas (Amendment) Act.
1938   Unemployment reached two million, but was countered by rearmament.
1939   Six million trade union members.
       3 September, Second World War began for Britain.

Further Reading

It is rare for books to combine the twin features of industrial relations and economic performance – most important studies focus either on the one or the other. Students wishing to read more widely than the present volume are therefore recommended to 'pick and mix' from the following:

1 Volumes on Economic History

An excellent introduction to Britain's economic history, 1900–45, is provided by the relevant chapters in **Charles More**, *The Industrial Age: Economy and Society in Britain, 1750–1985* (Longman 1989), while **Stephen Constantine**, *Unemployment in Britain between the Wars* (Longman 1980) gives a stimulating introduction to one aspect of Britain's inter-war economy.

More specialised works on the economy include the following: **Sidney Pollard**, *The Development of the British Economy, 1914–1990* (Edward Arnold 1992) – a 500-page textbook by one of the experts. **H.W. Richardson**, *Economic Recovery in Britain 1932–39* (Weidenfeld 1967) – a controversial study which stresses the positive aspects of Britain's performance in the 1930s. In contrast, **B.W.E. Alford**, *Depression and Recovery? British Economic Growth 1918–39* (Macmillan 1972) looks more sceptically at the problems of the inter-war years. Although it is too short to provide proper explanations, it is rich in bibliographical references.

On the debate on Keynes and the 'Treasury view', two books are well worth consulting: **Robert Skidelsky**, *Politicians and the Slump* (Penguin 1970) and **Peter Clarke**, *The Keynesian Revolution in the Making* (Oxford University Press 1988). A comparison between them is instructive. Skidelsky was writing at a time when it was widely believed that Keynes had 'solved' the problem of unemployment, while Clarke, writing so much later, is far less convinced of this and therefore far less critical of politicians.

2 Volumes on Industrial Relations

Henry Pelling, *A History of British Trade Unionism* (Penguin 1963) is still the most readable account, although it is now out of date on many issues.

Much more up to date but very short is **John Lovell**, *British Trade Unions, 1875–1933* (Macmillan 1977). Far more detailed (600 pages compared to 75) is **H.A. Clegg**, *A History of British Trade Unions since 1889, vol. 2 1911–33* (Clarendon 1985). **Alan Fox**, *History and Heritage: the social origins of the British industrial relations system* (Allen and Unwin 1985) is another large-scale survey.